A fascinating account of 500 years of Nevis History. Vince Hubbard has unequalled knowledge of Naval Warfare which raged between England, France and Spain in the 17th and 18th centuries, when each vied for control of the sugar islands and the huge wealth they gave.

Ian Church, Chairman of the Board (Retired)
Church's Shoes Ltd.
Whilton, Daventry, Northhants, England

*V*incent Hubbard has done a wonderful job weaving together the stories and accounts of Nevis's complex history into a delightful narrative. While the political and military history of Nevis is set forth with great accuracy, Hubbard does not lose sight of what makes Nevis such an extraordinary place — her people. The sometimes comical and sometimes tragic stories of Nevisians make this an excellent book.

Samuel M. Wilson
Department of Anthropology
University of Texas Austin, Texas USA

*H*ubbard presents the history of Nevis in a clear and informative way, while at the same time catching the romance and drama of the island's past. This interesting chronology of the frequent hurricanes that swept the island serve as a good reminder ... that we can yet expect some nasty blows from nature .... Visitors to Nevis, as well as those who live there, will find the book quite valuable. It is a keepsake.

Col. Charles M. Hansen
US Army (Retired)
Sausilito, Califomia USA

*H*aving an interest in anthropology, I was fascinated by the articles which related to the original habitation of the islands, and the unusual statue which appears to haunt the reader at the end in an enigmatic fashion.

James Clark, Managing Director
Fenchurch Trust Limited
Jersey, Channel Islands, UK

A must-read for Nevis old-timers and first-time visitors alike. History buffs will enjoy the colorful descriptions of the Arawaks and cannibalistic Caribs, Captain John Smith's rest stop in Nevis on the way to found the colony of Virginia, Lord Horatio Nelson's marriage to a local resident, the first American Naval victory near Nevis in 1799, Alexander Hamilton's ancestry, and the rise and fall of the sugar economy. Vacationers will learn more about landmarks such as Cottle Church, the Treasury Building and the Bath Hotel, the first resort in the Caribbean with possibly the first golf course in the Western Hemisphere. As a lawyer, I particularly enjoyed the references to Lord Nelson's lawsuit. I have been trying to explain to friends for 15 years why Nevis is so fascinating; now I can send them Mr. Hubbard's book.

Alice Young, Esq., Partner
Milbank, Tweed, Hadley & McCloy
New York, New York USA

I have read Swords, Ships and Sugar with great interest. A superb job. I found it particularly interesting to learn of the vastly different background of Nevis, compared to the Bahamas.

Robert E. Cordes, President
Management & Service Company Limited
Freeport, Bahamas

Swords, Ships and Sugar

A History of Nevis to 1900

An Illustrated Third Edition

"The scale of things has changed, and it is difficult now to conceive of how those neglected and unprosperous islands, many of them hardly bigger than the Isle of Wight, could ever loomed so large in the eyes of people and governments. Yet so it was; therefore to ignore the West Indies is to get a lopsided and unhistorical view of the mercantilist empire of the eighteenth century."

War and Trade in the West Indies, 1739-1763; Richard Pares, 1936

Cover Photograph: *Constellation vs L' Insurgente*
Depicts the victorious first battle of the United States Navy in
the waters of Nevis on February 9, 1799. Photo courtesy of
Department of Defense, Still Media Records Center, Washing-
ton, D.C., Rear Admiral John W. Schmidt.

Swords, Ships and Sugar

A History of Nevis to 1900
An Illustrated Third Edition

Vincent K. Hubbard

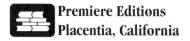

Premiere Editions
Placentia, California

For information, contact:
Premiere Editions
909 E. Yorba Linda Blvd., Suite H-2400
Placentia, California 92670 U.S.A.
Fax: (714) 572-3868

Edited by Irene Gresick
Designed by Karen Vitkus
Illustrations on pages 31, 58, 73 by Nan Becker
Photographs on pages 15, 18, 24, 61, 74, 79, 92, 95,
    Courtesy, Elizabeth Bilinski
Photographs on pages x, xii, 8, 54, 64, 65, 72, 88, 94, 97, 98, 108
    Courtesy, Museum of Nevis History, Charlestown

Printed in the United States of America

First Edition, November, 1992
Illustrated Second Edition, February, 1993
Illustrated Third Edition, October, 1993

Library of Congress Catalog Card Number: 93-85690
ISBN:0-9633818

This book is
dedicated to the
people of Nevis.

Proceeds to benefit
The Nevis Historical and Conservation Society.

Some funds to defray printing expense for the third edition of this book were
made available through British Government Heads of Mission Gifts.

Alexander Hamilton, founding father of the United States of America, and
first Secretary of the Treasury, was born in Charlestown. His birthplace
now houses the Museum of Nevis History and the House of Assembly.

Contents

Clay Ghaut windmill, built in 1795, was used until 1940. It was the last mill to operate in the Caribbean. When this photograph was taken in 1934, the original wooden gears (made of <u>lignun vitae</u> wood) and iron rollers were still going strong. The sails of the mill are being furled by the men climbing the vane.

Acknowledgements

There is insufficient space to thank everyone who helped with this work, but I would like to give special mention to the following:

David and Joan Robinson of The Museum of Nevis History, Charlestown; Dr. Samuel Wilson of the University of Texas, USA; Col. Charles Hansen of California, USA, Allen Mardis, Jr. and H.B. Hubbell of Connecticut, USA; Don Crandall and Marion Wheeler of Montserrat, BWI; Dr. Frank Paddock (deceased) of Massachusetts, USA; Herb Taylor of Ontario, Canada; Clive Mitchell of Richmond, Surrey, UK; Joyce Gordon of Devon, UK; Brent Wilson of the VSO; and David Rollinson, Pam Barry, Richard Lupinacci and Conrad Smithen of Nevis.

Main Street, Charlestown, circa 1890. Building on left is now Evelyn's Drug store; Longstone building is on the right.

Foreword

I doubt there are 36 square miles anywhere on this planet which have seen more dramatic action, wealth and poverty, adversity and triumph over adversity than has the island of Nevis. In the last 500 years, three distinctly different racial groups have controlled it — native Indians, Europeans, and Africans.

Sometimes they clashed, sometimes they competed and other times they cooperated. These groups have interacted to produce a unique society which, after years of hardship and economic decline, is now undergoing a renaissance. The purpose of this book is to pull together for the first time the bits and pieces of Nevis' history into a coherent whole. In the future, additional material will very likely be discovered and new stories will unfold.

St. Thomas

Tortola

Anguilla

St. John

St. Maarten

Saba

Barbuda

Puerto Rico

St. Croix

St. Barths

Statia

Antigua

St. Kitts

NEVIS

Montserrat

Guadeloupe

Dominica

Martinique

St. Lucia

St. Vincent

The Grenadines

Barbados

Grenada

Tobago

Trinidad

Courtesy, Nevis Tourism Office
Charlestown, Nevis, West Indies (809) 469-5521

Volcanoes and Rainfall | 1

In geological terms, Nevis in its present configuration is a relatively new island. Nevis Peak is approximately 980,000 years of age, but older rocks have been found elsewhere on the island. Nevis has been home to at least thirteen volcanoes at different times in its history. Saddle Hill and Hurricane Hill bear traces of some of them which have substantially weathered away. During the last Ice Age when the sea level was around 200 feet lower than at present, Nevis, St. Kitts, Statia and Saba were one island and other connected island chains may have existed throughout the Antilles.

What is important about Nevis Peak and its volcanic origin is the relationship it has to the island weather and plant life. Volcanic materials break down rapidly into rich soil, and in the Caribbean, a peak of over 3,000 feet is required to create sufficient rainfall for substantial plant growth. This fact is clearly evident by comparing plant life on Nevis to that of predominately sedimentary islands such as Anguilla, Barbuda and to a lesser extent, Antigua, all of which are flatter and drier islands.

The plant and animal life existing on Nevis today is totally unlike that which was here when Europeans first arrived. Citrus, mangoes (brought from India), breadfruit (brought from Tahiti), bananas, yams, plantain, okra and pigeon peas (from Africa), cassava (brought by Indians from South America), sugar, coconut, and most ornamental flowers all came from outside.

Grapefruit originated somewhere in the Caribbean when oranges brought originally from Spain crossed naturally with the Shaddock. The Shaddock is a large, rounded and not very juicy fruit from the far east and was brought to the Caribbean in the 17th century by an English sea captain named Shaddock. Barbados claims to be the spot where grapefruit first came into being, but it is unproven.

It is, in fact, difficult to determine what plant and animal species were actually on the island before the 17th century. Parrots are now extinct in Nevis while the vervet (African green) monkeys were brought in so early as to be considered a pest by 1725. The mongoose was brought here in the late 19th century to control rats and the crapaud (<u>bufus marinus</u> toad) was imported about the same time to control the sugar cane beetle. Honey bees were brought from Europe in the 17th century.

Indians and Early Exploration

Christopher Columbus anchored overnight at Nevis on his second voyage to the New World on November 11, 1493. He named it San Martin, as it was sighted on St. Martin's day.

By 1540, the island's name appeared on maps as "Nieves" in Spanish, meaning "snow." That was a contraction of the name "Santa Maria de las Nieves", the origin of which was a miraculous summer snowstorm in Spain.[1] Evidently, Mount Nevis' cloud cover sometimes appeared similar to a snow cap to sailors. An early description of the island states the mountain was "...covered with clouds of congregation fantastical."[2]

The first written account yet discovered of a visit to Nevis was in June 1603, when Captain Bartholemew Gilbert of Plymouth, England, sailed here with a work party of 20 men and boys for the purpose of cutting <u>lignum vitae</u> wood. His vessel was the 50-ton bark <u>Elizabeth of London</u>. There is no mention of sighting Indians, but they indicated there were signs of trees having been cut by others (probably Europeans). In slightly over two weeks, they cut, trimmed and loaded twenty tons of wood.

This was a formidable task. <u>Lignum vitae</u> is so dense it won't float and a nail can't be driven into it without first drilling a hole. Termites will not eat it and cutting it must have been a difficult job indeed. The men found plenty to eat, however. The account relates that on June 19, 1603:

> This day in the Evening some went with the Boate unto the shore, and brought on boord a Tortoyse so big that foure men could not get her into the Boate but tied her fast by one legge unto the Boat, and so towed her to the ship, when they had her by the ship, it was no easie matter to get her on board. ...This day at night we opened our Tortoyse, which had in her about 500 Egges, excellent sweet meat, and so is the whole fish.[3]

There were so many sea turtles in both Nevis and St. Kitts the men complained that when they cast nets for fish, turtles were continually caught in them. They caused the nets to burst and allowed the fish to escape.

Leaving Nevis, they stopped a day in St. Kitts and then sailed onward to Virginia. There, Captain Gilbert intended to search for the lost settlers of Roanoke Island who had attempted unsuccessfully to establish an English colony in 1587.

In Virginia, misfortune caught up with them. Captain Gilbert, Thomas Canner (Gent.), Masters Mate Richard Harrison, Ship's Doctor Henry Kenton, and a Dutchman named Derricke went ashore in "the Bay of Chesepian" [Chesapeake] and were attacked and murdered by Indians within sight of the boat. It was sadly ironic, as the ship's first landfall was at St. Lucia in the West Indies where the Indians were friendly, traded with them, and shared the beer carried by the sailors.

Captain John Smith with three ships stopped in Nevis for five days to rest on his way from England in 1607 to establish the colony of Virginia in North America. Following prevailing winds and ocean currents, early sailing vessels coming from Europe would be carried to this area as was Columbus in 1493 when he "discovered" Nevis. It seems certain that Smith was aware of the existence of the thermal waters of the Bath Stream and believed it was a favorable place for his crew to recuperate after the long voyage across the Atlantic.

Smith stated that the island was heavily wooded from the shore to the top of the mountain except for an area of sand dunes on the southeast side, and there were great numbers of fish, fowl, and "conies" available for food. "Conie" is an Elizabethan term for rabbits, but the animals he called "conies" were probably hutia, a cat-sized rodent similar to a large Guinea Pig which is still found in Dominica and South America. They are eaten today by Indians and originally may have been brought to Nevis by them.

Smith found his men were very much revived by their stay here. He attributed it to the curative powers of the Bath Stream waters. It is today believed the sulphur content of the water may act upon the body in a way similar to the antibiotic sulfa-drugs developed in the 1940's. Just as likely is that simply bathing in hot water after nearly two months at sea, eating fresh food and fruit and resting combined to strengthen them for their voyage onward to Virginia.

Smith praised the Bath Stream, saying it cured gunpowder burns and the serious skin irritations his men had gotten from the sap of a tree which resembled a fig but was undoubtedly the poisonous manchineel which still grows here, usually near the sea.

To protect his men from the possibility of Indian attack, a guarded camp was established. The Indians apparently lived on the opposite windward side of the island, but some of Smith's men on an exploration expedition encountered an Indian hunting party somewhere inland. Each group ran from the other, however, and there was no bloodshed.[4]

In 1608, Robert Harcourt stopped in Nevis for a brief time on his way back from Guyana in South America to England. He and his men bathed in the Bath Stream and Harcourt claimed the waters cured his cough and declared they would cure leprosy as well.[5]

As notable as the Bath Stream waters seemed to be for curing ailments, other early visitors did not speak well of the Nevis water supply. In 1684, William Hacke wrote:

> The fresh water on this island is not very good, it is so hot that you can scarce keep ye hand in it, the Inhabitants save raine water & keep it in Cisterns made of stone for theire necessary ocasions.[6]

The first human settlement of Nevis occurred possibly around 2,000 B.C., as pre-ceramic Indians worked their way up the Antilles chain from South America. People had moved into the Greater Antilles somewhat earlier, probably from Central America. Archaeologists are still trying to piece together exactly where the first Indian inhabitants of Cuba and Hispanola came from, but it is clear that they arrived there between 5,000 and 3,000 B.C.

Significant finds of carved basalt stone items attributed to the early Saladoid period [Arawaks] have been found on the west side of the island on the site of the Four Seasons Golf Course. These items, unfortunately removed from Nevis, could be over 2,000 years old.

The Arawaks seem to have settled on the windward (east) side of the island. They brought with them the ability to make a type of red painted pottery with white markings which dates as early as a few centuries B.C.

For a long time it was thought that warlike Carib Indians may have captured Nevis and the other Leewards from the Arawaks. Recently, however, scholars have found that the Caribs and Arawaks were closely related in language and culture. Although the people of the lesser Antilles did sometimes raid Puerto Rico and the larger islands, it appears the people we call Caribs and Arawaks had been living together for many centuries before the arrival of Columbus.[7]

The Caribs were termed "cannibals" by the Europeans, as they had the ritualistic habit of eating parts of slain enemies' bodies. Because of this cannibalistic trait, the Spanish were allowed to enslave Caribs but not (theoretically) the Arawaks. Following this ruling, many Arawaks found themselves redefined as Caribs overnight. As a result, it is very difficult to tell whether the Carib-Arawak distinction truly existed or whether it was a product of the Europeans' arrival. At any rate, Caribs battled Europeans in many places throughout the Caribbean, including Nevis.

One explanation of the small numbers of Indians found in Nevis by the English may have to do with pearl diving in a faraway place. In the early 16th century, pearls were discovered on the island of Cubagua off the Venezuelan coast. The Spanish in the meantime had designated the Leewards and Windwards "useless islands" as far as settlement was concerned, and allowed the capturing of Indians from those islands for pearl diving in Cubagua. [8]

They were forced to spend 16 hours a day diving from 20 to 70 feet deep and held rocks in their arms to carry them quickly to the bottom. Needless to say, they did not live long. In 1520 angry Caribs retaliated by attacking the island in war canoes and slaughtering the Spaniards. That attack, combined with the overfishing of pearls, ended the trade. It is quite likely that Indians from Nevis perished in Cubagua.

Whatever the reasons, by the time Europeans came here to settle, there were few if any Indians left. Disease, enslavement, and random Spanish attacks in retaliation for Carib raids on Puerto Rico had taken their toll. However, we have found in 17th century records indications that small numbers were working as slaves on plantations here as late as the 1680's. The narrow faces and high cheekbones of some contemporary Nevisians may reflect an Indian heritage.

Archaeological investigations in Nevis have given us some indications of how its Indian inhabitants lived. It has been estimated that in the period 500 to 600 A.D. the Indian population probably exceeded 1,000 and could have been considerably higher, perhaps as high as 5,000. Twenty-two confirmed Indian sites from varying time periods have been located on the island, most on the windward side and all being near the sea. An analysis of bones found in burial sites indicate that the primary portion of the diet (about 60%) consisted of shellfish and reef fish. This fact would seem to indicate the Indians dived on the reefs which encircle the windward side of the island. Cassava was grown and its flour prepared as cakes on clay grills which had a distinctive criss-cross pattern, preventing the cakes from sticking to the grill. Fragments of these grills are common in Indian sites on the island.

As in other Caribbean islands, Indian dwelling houses appear to have had thatch roofs and were probably either small and conical in shape or large rectangular communal buildings, or both. Post holes have been found in several sites here indicating that some of the buildings, whatever the type of construction, were supported by large logs. The early colonial name "Indian Castle" might have indicated the presence of a large Indian structure in that southeastern area of Nevis at the time of European settlement. The English during that era used the term "castle" to indicate a fortress or an imposing building.

Present in the dwelling sites are tool fragments made from stone and conch shell as well as chunks of flint. Flint is not native to Nevis and had to be imported, as were small polished granite beads also discovered in the sites. There was evidently waterborn commerce with distant places. However, lacking any written information about Nevis' indigenous population, we can only make educated guesses based on archaeological discoveries.

Storm clouds forming over the ruins of the Bath Hotel, as seen from the Main Road, Circa 1900.

Hurricanes | 2

Hurricanes have been and continue to be a scourge in the Caribbean. The word "hurricane" itself derives from the name of the Carib Indian deity "Hunrakan" who, according to legend, sent the winds when he was angry. Europeans exploring the Caribbean soon confronted the fury of these storms which exceeded in force any they had experienced outside of this region.

The destruction wrought by hurricanes in Nevis has been vast through the years. In the past, there was no early warning system or indication of the force or path of the storm. Seamen and residents of the area soon learned to see the signs in nature, however. A period of hot, still weather usually from July through October and numerous fish visible beneath the clear surface of the sea were early indications of an approaching storm. If large swells subsequently appeared on a windless day, the storm was getting closer. Most 17th century buildings in Nevis were built of wood one and a half stories high only, because of "hurri-canes."

As bad as a hurricane was on land, for sailors at sea it meant sheer terror and a likelihood of death. At the best of times the wind-driven sailing ships of the past were hard to maneuver. In a hurricane they would put to sea, if they could, and run before the storm to wherever the wind carried them. There have been several proven instances of sailing ships in the Caribbean running 500 to 600 miles during a hurricane. In port, the anchors and cables would usually not hold and the vessel would be driven ashore and wrecked. Often ships were unable to leave harbors because of adverse winds and currents. Even if a ship succeeded in putting to sea its chances of survival were marginal. Under the stress of wind and heavy seas, the vessel could leak and sink if the pumps proved unable to deal with the water. It could also be capsized or be driven onto a reef, especially at night when lack of visibility prevented evasive action. Many ships have been lost in Nevis' waters, the vast majority during hurricanes.

Hurricanes were far more frequent in the 17th and 18th centuries (26 in the 18th century) in Nevis than in the 19th and 20th centuries. Only three have struck the island in this century; 1924, 1928, and Hugo in 1989. In the early 18th Century, every Sunday in July, August and September was a Fast Day in the Anglican Churches. If no hurricanes ravaged the island by the beginning of October, the first Sunday in October was a day of Thanksgiving. [9] The following list, derived from various sources, may not be complete nor totally accurate (since 1825 records have not been compiled in such detail as before). However, the number and ferocity of past hurricanes should give us pause to think of what the future could bring to Nevis.

Nevis experienced hurricanes of widely varying strength in the following years:

1623, 1642 (3)

1650 (2), 1651, 1652, 1665, 1666, 1667 (2); in the second storm, nearly all houses were blown down, "the inhabitants sought shelter from its fury by throwing themselves flat on the ground in the fields."

1669, 1680, 1681 (3); in the third storm, "Captaine Cushing, master, and Captaine Clark, from New-England, having thirty or more horses on board, lost twenty-five as he was coming into Nevis."

1707 (Nevis "nearly ruined")

1718, 1728, 1733, 1737, 1740, 1747 (2; eight ships wrecked in second storm in Nevis)

1751, 1754, 1758, 1765, 1766, 1772 (3; after first storm, "Nevis had scarcely a house left standing"; second s t o r m followed three days later)

1775, 1776, 1779 (at Charlestown, it "disbursed" a blockading French Fleet of 38 warships; some sank)

1780 (the "Great Hurricane" — the worst in History. 22,000 estimated killed in the Caribbean, which included over 6,000 sailors drowned when warring British, French and Spanish fleets were destroyed; Nevis was spared the strongest winds. Elsewhere bark was stripped from trees, sustained wind speed is estimated to have been well over 200 m.p.h.)

1785, 1790   (in Nevis, 20 ships wrecked, new Hamilton Estate Great House destroyed)

1792 (2), 1793, 1811, 1813, 1819, 1835 ("devastating")

1867, 1899 (powerful; coast road badly damaged).[10]

An extremely rare book written by the Reverend Robert Robertson of St. Paul's Church in Charlestown giving details of the powerful 1733 hurricane has been called the best account of a tropical hurricane ever written. He noted that between St. Kitts and Nevis, 2,000 hogsheads of sugar were lost and the cane fields were destroyed. The writer describes a tornado which occurred during the storm:

The house I live in is not above 200 yards east from the Sea; and I saw one of those Gyres, or Whirls, at no great distance from me to the Northward, carrying, and at the same time circulating within its Compass, an immense quantity of Cane - Trash, Bushes, and Boughs of Trees; I followed it with my Eye into the Sea where it toss'd, or drew up the Water to a vast Height into the Air, but the rain falling thicker than before, hinder'd me from following it long. [11]

Regarding the fate of shipping caught in the storm, he noted that some sailors from Montserrat had been blown from there to Nevis and wrecked at Indian Castle, and "a few" survived. In addition, he made the following observations:

Captain Payne, in a Bristol Snow from Guinea, having got its Loading, put out; but the vessel, being crazy, sunk down between St. Eustace and St. Martin's; himself and all the crew were drown'd, except the Boatswain and two sailors, who swam to a Bermudas sloop, which had overset at a small Distance from them, and saved themselves on her Bottom, as her own crew also did...

One Partridge, an Inhabitant of this Place, put out in his Scooner with a Son of Mr. Sheppard's, and overset near the Nagg's Head, as we suppose; the Scooner has since been seen, Bottom up, between St. Christopher's and St. Bartholomew's. The Castle-Shallop [a small open vessel similar to a present-day lighter] belonging to the Estate of Sir William Stapleton, had been with a Load of Sugar to Basterre, from whence the three Negroes, that sailed her, ventur'd out in the Storm, and to the wonder of many, kept the Sea, till they reach'd Anguilla, where they were glad to run her ashore to save themselves, and are now return'd safe in another Vessel with the Rigging, etc. of the Shallop.[12]

A Spanish Lake

From the time of Columbus' discovery of Nevis in 1493 until 1671, Spain claimed not only Nevis but all the Caribbean Islands. Imperial Spain was then the richest country on earth and the world's most powerful maritime nation. The Spanish never settled but probably did explore Nevis, as did early navigators from other nations. At that time, the Caribbean was a "Spanish Lake" and ships from other nations ventured into it at their peril.

In 1620, two Spanish Men-of-War, one of 20 and the other of 16 guns, lay in wait for trespassers on the western side of Nevis. They encountered a small eight-gun English ship, Margaret and John of London, when she stopped for water on her way from England to Virginia.[13]

Before reaching Nevis, Margaret and John had made landfall in Martinique and there picked up six shipwrecked French sailors who had been living among the Indians for six months. The Frenchmen warned them that two Spanish warships had been sighted and could still be in the vicinity. Nevis was a common stopover for English and Dutch vessels bound for North America, according to the account of this incident. The Spanish knew this and their ships were fitted to appear to be Dutch. Margaret and John anchored and the decision was made to send a boat out to hail the other two vessels. Captain Anthony Chester suspected they might be the Spaniards he had been warned about, so he anchored in a position to make a quick getaway if necessary.

A London grocer named Thomas Hothersall, a passenger migrating to Virginia with his family, had the bad luck to be fluent in both Spanish and Dutch. Much against his wishes, he was ordered into the longboat as spokesman to hail the unidentified ships. After exchanging a few words at the maximum possible hailing distance, Hothersall determined to his satisfaction the ships were Spanish and advised the sailors to row back to Margaret and John as quickly as they could.

When the longboat came about, both of the unidentified ships ran up the Spanish flag and soldiers kneeling in the gunwales opened fire on it with harquebusses [very long muskets with a flare at the end of the muzzle]. Hothersall reported that a ball passed through his jerkin [a sleeveless jacket] and the bottom of the boat and he stopped up the leak with his handkerchief. Both the Spanish vessels and Margaret and John began warping so they could fire broadsides at one another while the longboat raced toward its mother ship under heavy Spanish fire.

Captain Chester attempted to escape, but the anchor had fouled on the bottom and could not be lifted. Sailors were out in another longboat desperately trying to free it when one Spanish ship came alongside the helpless Margaret and John, fired a broadside into her, and then attempted a boarding.

The Spanish Captain ("the brave cavalier") led his men over the rail and was shot dead as he crossed it. On the deck, the English resisted in fierce hand-to-hand fighting. Using muskets, pistols, cutlasses and swords, they succeeded in fending off the attack. In the meantime, sailors had cut the anchor cable and Captain Chester sped away from Nevis with the two Spanish warships in pursuit. The faster Spanish warships overtook him on the high seas and one closed to attempt a second boarding. Again Margaret and John put up spirited resistance and repelled the attack. Following this second failed attempt, the Spanish broke off action and headed for Saba.

With their overwhelmingly superior firepower, the Spaniards could have simply shot the smaller vessel to pieces and sunk or boarded her. Why they didn't is not known. Margaret and John continued onward to Virginia with ten dead and 19 wounded out of the 109 men and women she carried. The dead included three of the shipwrecked French sailors.

Another fatality was Lawrence Bohun [Boon], recently appointed Physician General of Jamestown, Virginia, and badly needed in the young colony. He was shot through the head and died instantly as he emerged from a hatch onto the deck in the thick of the fight. [14]

European Settlement of Nevis

In 1628, the English officially sent colonists from St. Kitts to Nevis where they established Jamestown as the island's capital. Unofficially, however, it is likely Nevis was first settled as early as 1625. A British Commission of Enquiry in 1826 set the date of Nevis' settlement as 1625 for the purpose of determining which laws were in force in the colony. In addition, it was English custom to name a capital of a new colony after the reigning monarch and King James died in 1625.[15]

The commander of the first official settlers of Nevis was Captain Anthony Hilton, sent from St. Kitts by Sir Thomas

Courtesy , Elizabeth Bilinski

Built before 1650, the Newcastle Redoubt protected early inhabitants from Carib Indian attack. It is probably the oldest standing structure in the Commonwealth Caribbean.

Warner. Shortly afterward, Hilton was accused of stealing all the island's tobacco crop and possible piracy, and from the few existing records, the accusations appear to be well founded. It should be remembered that many of the early English colonists in the Caribbean were adventurers and not of the highest character. A waggish observer in the 17th century West Indies wrote that when new colonies were established, the first thing the Spanish did was to build a church, the Dutch to build a fort, and the English to build a tavern. Nonetheless, by 1642 the population of Nevis was estimated to be 10,000. The population of the Colony of Virginia that year was estimated to be only 8,000.

The proprietary colony was financed privately by the Earl of Carlisle with the backing of the Crown. Carlisle rented all the "Charriby Islands" from the King of England for an annual rate of 100 pounds and a white horse. In 1664, the Crown took over direct control and Carlisle is reported to have died in poverty. Nevis was unusual among the Leewards in that many of its early settlers were from aristocratic English Royalist families in the Civil War who had fled to the Colonies when Charles I was beheaded.[16]

When the Crown took control of Nevis, the local established Government became a bicameral legislature with a Council and Assembly. The Assembly consisted of locally elected property owners and the Council was appointed by the Crown through the Lords of Trade and Plantations at first, and later through the Colonial Office. In general, the Assembly's laws could not extend for more than one year and the Council's laws extended for over one year. The President of the Council served as Governor of Nevis except during the period in the late 17th and early 18th century when Nevis was the seat of the Leeward Islands Colony. The Colonial Governor of the Leewards then also served as Governor of Nevis.

The laws of the Nevis Council had to be approved by the Crown and because of that they all had a preamble which explained in detail just why the law was being passed. These laws give a good picture of early life on the island. For instance, a 1680 law began with the statement, "Whereas, the Wells and Springs of Charles Town are filled with noxious stincks and odors..." An early anti-pollution law, it went on to prohibit "boiling pots and dressing victuals" in the streets of Charlestown, as the residue was poured onto the ground and percolated into the water supply.

Predictably, the Spanish took issue with English settlement of lands the former claimed as their own. In 1629, Admiral Don Fadrique de Toledo arrived from Spain, on his way to Brazil with a fleet of 36 ships, drove off an English squadron of nine vessels under the command of Captain Henry Hawley, and destroyed the English settlements first in Nevis and then St. Kitts.[17] Captain Hawley later became Governor of Barbados and died when, in a drunken condition, he fell down the steps of a tavern in Bridgetown, breaking his neck.

At the time, clearing Nevis for agricultural purposes was being done by indentured servants which included many Roman Catholic Irish. They appeared not to be happy with their lot on Nevis. Many deserted and left with the Spanish. Some even struck out swimming to the Spanish ships in order to escape.

Some of the uprooted settlers were transported to the infamous island of Tortuga, north of Hispanola, where they joined the worst buccaneer and pirate colony in the entire Caribbean. The somewhat shady Captain Hilton was one of that group and soon became Governor of Tortuga, but had disputes with the French "corsairs" already living there. The disputes ended when the Spanish attacked the island and killed Hilton and everyone else they could find.

Consecrated in 1633, St. Thomas Lowland Church was the first Anglican Church in the Caribbean, serving the lost capital of Jamestown.

Religious Conflicts | 3

Due to the desertion of the Irish Roman Catholics and ongoing conflicts between Protestants and Catholics, laws were passed in 1703 forbidding Roman Catholics from settling in the Leeward Islands. It was feared they might defect to Catholic Spain or France in the then current war of the Spanish Succession. Protestant England and Holland were fighting Catholic Spain and France. The fact that the very able Leeward Islands Governor, Sir William Stapleton, had been a Roman Catholic Irishman seemed not to matter. When these laws were repealed in 1752 throughout the Leeward Islands, the Nevis Assembly refused to honor the repealing act and the session discussing the matter degenerated into a riot. The Leeward Islands Governor in Antigua compelled compliance by threatening to send troops to Nevis.[18]

In 1658, laws were passed excluding Quaker settlers as well. The Quakers simply refused to bear arms under any circumstances. In 1676, it was noted by Governor Sir William Stapleton that:

> They will neither watch nor ward against the Caribbee Indians, whose treacherous and barbarous murders, rapes and enormities discourage the planters in the Leeward Islands more than anything else.[19]

In 1655, Quaker settlers under their founder, George Fox, had been turned away from Nevis after leaving Barbados. A ship's Captain knowingly landing a Quaker in Nevis in 1661 could be fined 5,000 pounds of sugar. The fine was later increased to 10,000 pounds. In today's money, the latter sum would equal approximately US $25,000.00. Governor Sir Charles Wheler stated the reason for passage of the laws was that every able-bodied European man between 14 and 60 had to join the militia and Nevis was beset by enemies on every side. In 1674, Wheler complained he could raise only 700 militia and needed every one.

So strong were the anti-Quaker feelings here that a law was passed declaring that anyone appearing before a public body wearing a hat (Quaker men customarily wore a broad-brimmed black hat at all times) would be fined 500 pounds of sugar or imprisoned for one month. A Quaker named Humphry Highwood complained about the law before a judge while wearing his hat and in lieu of the fine and costs was imprisoned for two months and three weeks.

In 1667, a Constable and officers of the militia raided a Quaker Meeting House where a religious service was in progress and arrested the male participants. Thirteen were imprisoned. The fourteenth was a slave named Toney, "... which Negro, a sober and sensible Man, they put in irons, and much abused him."[20]

In 1675, another Quaker named John Brown and two others interrupted a service at St. George's Church in Gingerland (then called New-River Church), rising to their feet during a moment of silence and accusing the Reverend John Lawson of being "a man of iniqity" who would not preach unless first being paid. They were immediately set in the stocks and then jailed. Reverend Lawson sued Brown for libel and slander and damages in the amount of 100,000 pounds of sugar. Lawson won the lawsuit but was awarded no damages. In spite of being a Quaker, Brown owned a slave who was seized to cover his master's costs resulting from this court action.

On April 7, 1678, Brown was removed from jail under a Royal Warrant issued by the Governor banishing him from

Nevis and ordering him to be placed on board the bark Hope, to be taken to "the island of Long-Island or any other place where there are Quakers." Following removal from his cell, he was "beaten with a great cane" by Provost Marshal (Sheriff) Caesar Rodney and forcibly placed on board the vessel as a crowd watched.

In 1705, restrictions against Quakers were repealed by the Nevis Council, but less than a century later, no Quakers remained in the Caribbean.

Jews were welcomed in Nevis. In the 17th century, they were suffering religious persecution in Brazil and many fled to the Protestant English and Dutch Caribbean Islands. They were restricted to being merchants and could not own land, but later some became planters. They and Dutch traders brought with them the secret of how to crystallize sugar, which the Portuguese and Spanish had invented and attempted to keep for themselves. This was the process of boiling the cane juice in a line of coppers of decreasing size, removing impurities and adding lime, and at the end pouring the thickened syrup in cooling pans to crystallize. The line of coppers in boiling houses for years was called a "Spanish train."

Part of the synagogue in Charlestown, dating from the 17th century, has been rediscovered behind the Administration Building, and the nearby remains of the Jewish cemetery in Charlestown are still maintained today. The stones are dated between 1670 and 1758 and bear inscriptions in Portuguese, Hebrew and English.

By 1678, Nevis had the largest Jewish population in the English Leewards. In the 1720's, an Anglican priest estimated one-quarter of the white population of St. Paul's Parish, Charlestown, was Jewish.

In 1787, Bishop Thomas Coke of the newly organized Methodist Church visited Nevis, but received a cool reception. He was surprised to find when he returned two years later that interest had grown and people were prepared to support the church. Within a decade, the membership had grown to 400 (90% black) and several chapels had been established around the island. By 1797, the number of Methodists in Nevis exceeded that of any of the other Leewards.[21] They were, however, regarded with suspicion by some planters as the church was believed to be against slavery. This was a fact, but the church was not strident about its beliefs and its ministry to the slave population was well regarded by some prominent people, including the Nisbet family of Nisbet Plantation and Admiralty Judge Ward. On several plantations, owners allowed Ministers to preach to slaves on a regular basis. Charles Wesley wrote in England that the life of a slave was hopeless by the nature of it, but that hope could be given by anticipation of the world to come.

In 1727, the Reverend Robert Robertson of St. Paul's Church in Nevis, wrote the Bishop of London an eloquent treatise of over 100 pages urging that more slaves should be baptized and given religious instruction. Robertson believed the Church of England was neglecting the slaves' spiritual welfare by not having sufficient clergy in the West India colonies to attend to these functions. He contended that the time to commence religious instruction was when slaves first arrived here. He noted that "scarcely one in fifteen" arrivals spoke the same African tongue. Therefore, they had to learn English immediately in order to communicate and he believed that religious instruction should be given along with language instruction. He suggested that promising University students in England be indentured for a period of seven years, sent to the islands, and paid by Government to give this instruction.

He went on to say that slaves needed Christian teaching as they were prone to "Laziness, Stealing, Stubbornness, Murmuring, Treachery, Lying, Drunkenness, and the like..." However, the slaves' perceived wickedness paled into relative insignificance next to that of the immigrating English, whose evils were so considerable that the existing clergy's time was completely filled dealing with them. Robertson discussed the white population of Nevis, declaring that "…the Mother-Nation now and then replenishes them with whole Ship-Loads of Pick-Pockets, Whores, Rogues, Vagrants, Thieves, Sodomites, and other Filth and Cut-Throats of Society." [21.1]

Religion was often not seriously practiced by many of these early inhabitants of Nevis. In 1671, Governor Wheler complained to the Lords of Trade and Plantations that "for the near forty Parishes" in all the Leeward Islands, he had as clergy only "a drunken sectary priest, a drunken priest, and a drunken parson with no orders." [22]

In 1704, it was reported that one of Nevis' most prominent planters died and his family paid the Anglican Priest at St. Paul's Church 500 "island" pounds (equalling in value 222 pounds, four shillings and five pence English money) to preach a "panegyric" at the burial service. The average annual salary of a priest at that time was between 75 and 125 pounds a year. [23] If it is possible to preach a sinner into heaven, that unidentified planter probably made it. In 1764, one William Tucket and several others were fined six pounds for rioting. In a drunken state, they had invaded the home of Edwin Thomas, rector of St. John's Church, shouting "damnation to all parsons."

In the 1790's, a despairing Methodist missionary wrote, "Women and drink drive all before them here." [24]

Spiked by the French in 1782, this ancient 12 pounder still stands sentinel at Fort Ashby.

The Collision of Empires | 4

It is difficult in today's context to understand why tiny Nevis was a focal point of European Imperial adventures in the 17th and 18th centuries. It was basically because of the vast riches generated for a time by Caribbean sugar production.

The commencement of cultivation of "King Sugar" completely changed Nevis. The first commercial agriculture here consisted of tobacco, cotton and indigo cultivated on small farms, but Virginia tobacco was of much better quality than that which could be grown in Nevis.

The Lords of Trade and Plantations in England theoretically controlled Nevis' agricultural production. In 1664, Nevis planters successfully petitioned Lord Willoughby, the Royal Governor then located in Barbados, for permission to grow sugar. What his lordship didn't know was that sugar had been unofficially grown on the island for some years and clandestinely exported in Dutch vessels. Records show that when England and Holland were at war in 1651, property of Dutch planters on Nevis was confiscated by the Crown and among the property seized was 101,000 pounds of sugar. The Dutch retaliated for this seizure in 1665 when the famous Admiral de Ruyter raided Nevis and captured 16 ships.

On May 28, 1673, the Dutch attacked Nevis again with a Fleet composed of nine men-of-war, six supply vessels, and 1,100 men under the command of Admiral Evertson. They had first attacked Montserrat, taking a merchant ship and killing a 14-year-old "cannon boy," but were ultimately driven away. It was the intention of the Dutch to capture any of the English Leewards which weren't well defended.

Nevis gave them a warm reception. The shore batteries fired on and hit some of the attacking vessels, killing the Captain and Quartermaster of one of them. Observers on shore noted Dutch sailors going over the sides of their warships with wooden plugs to stop up holes at the waterline made by Nevis' cannon. With that pounding, any idea of landing troops ended.

Seven Dutch pinnaces [small merchant ships] were then dispatched from the fleet carrying soldiers to board and capture English merchantmen anchored under protection of the shore batteries. As the Dutch were unable to invade they hoped at least to take some prize ships. However, the fire from Nevis' batteries was so accurate and intense that the attack on the merchantmen was called back and none were captured. [25]

The Dutch then withdrew from Nevis and raided St. Kitts, taking a French ship and killing five civilians and a soldier with cannon fire. Following that, they then landed on Saba and captured it. Saba remains Dutch to this day.

In 1655, General Robert Venables of England drew 300 recruits from Nevis and more from other islands to attack the Spanish in Hispanola and Puerto Rico. Both attacks failed largely because Venables' force was made up of men unsuitable for fighting. The European settlers and troops in the Caribbean were in many cases the dregs of society, classified by an English officer as "profane and debauched rogues and whores". [26] During that era, many criminals, vagrants and prostitutes were shipped to the West Indies from England.

Colonel Butler of Nevis, a Government Commissioner, went to St. Kitts to gain recruits for this force and in front of his own and French officers became so drunk that he fell from his horse and vomited, much to the amusement of the French.

General Venables' ragtag force failed in its mission to take Santo Domingo or San Juan, but went on to lightly defended Spanish Jamaica and captured it for Britain. In 1657, Leewards

Governor Luke Stokes of Nevis departed with 1,600 Nevisians, black and white, and settled in Jamaica. Although half of them died of disease, including Stokes, the settlement was ultimately successful. There is an historical link between the two islands going back almost 350 years to this embryonic settlement.

During this war between Spain and England, three Nevisians were swept up by events and had a hair-raising adventure. Thomas Bertonshere, William Clarke and Thomas Carter were captured at sea in 1654 by the Spanish "plate fleet" [10 to 15 heavily armed galleons which carried silver ("plata") to Spain once a year]. They were taken to Spain where they broke out of captivity and managed to escape the country concealed in a Dutch vessel sailing to Holland. They made their way from Holland to England in an English frigate which landed them on the Kentish coast, and from there they travelled overland to London. Upon arrival, they reported their story to Government authorities and declared the intent to return to Nevis by the first available ship. We do not know whether they arrived safely home or not, but one hopes so. It took 21 months from the time of their capture for them to reach London.[27]

The French and English for years fought for control of the Caribbean and the most frequent and serious attacks on Nevis were made by the French.

The Anglo-French rivalry sometimes had an amusing side. In 1679, neighboring St. Kitts was split between French and English control. The French had two frigates stationed in St. Kitts and the English had none in the area. That gave the French the run of the seas.

Protocol of the day required that a foreign ship entering a harbor had to strike her colors and in acknowledgment a cannon salute was fired by the land batteries. If a vessel failed to comply, a warning shot was fired across her bows. If that was not effective, worse could follow.

On the 29th of June 1679, a small French merchantman called a "flyboat," named La Sara de Rochelle, under the command of Captain Michel, was passing Fort Charles and failed to lower her flag as required. The gunners in the Fort duly fired the warning shot. Rather than responding as expected, "the impudent fellow" fired a cannon at the English flag flying over the Fort. That provoked angry return fire from Fort Charles which missed, and the French Captain, having effectively thumbed his nose at the English, bore off for St. Kitts. One can imagine he laughed all the way to Basseterre.

Governor Stapleton was furious. He wrote to the Lords of Trade and Plantations in England reporting the incident and requesting that a frigate be dispatched to Nevis in order to keep the French in line. He wrote, "It frets me to skin and bones to see such indignities heaped on the King's flag by their very merchantmen." His request was heard in England and a Frigate (the equivalent of a Destroyer in a modern Navy) was soon posted to Nevis.[28]

The presence of a Frigate did not stop a similar incident in 1700 which had a far more serious outcome. Three French ships of the line, the battleships of that age, sailed into Charlestown harbor under the command of Admiral de Modene. Evidently the vessels were expected, but de Modene failed to strike his colors and Fort Charles' gunners put a shot across the flagship's bow as she anchored. Evidently, Admiral de Modene was quite offended by this act. Yet, there was purpose to the protocol. Following the required actions assured both sides that the two nations were not at war. Communications were so slow in those days that a war could begin or end and one side or the other or both might be unaware of it. Following protocol assured all parties concerned that, as best they knew, peace prevailed.

Under a white flag of truce, a longboat was dispatched by the Governor of Nevis to de Modene to determine why he had not struck his colors. De Modene replied that it had been an oversight, France and Great Britain were not at war, and that in order to show his contrition he would fire a salute to Great Britain after Fort Charles fired its salute to France. His explanation was accepted, de Modene struck his colors, and a time was set for the salutes to be exchanged. Word spread quickly through-out Nevis and people of every station of life gathered at the Charlestown bayfront to witness this display of firepower. It would be impressive indeed — cannon of that day gave forth a long flash of orange flame from the muzzle, great clouds of dark gray smoke, and a boom like a clap of thunder when fired.

At the given hour, the ceremonial gunners at Fort Charles, having removed the shot from their cannon, fired their salute with blank charges. As soon as this was completed, de Modene ran out the guns from his flagship. Rather than firing a salute, he had purposely loaded his guns with shot and ball and fired a broadside into Fort Charles. Cannonballs and grape shot cut down many militiamen in the fort and before the rest could gather their wits and return fire, a second broadside was fired into the Fort by the ship.

As bad as this was, the other two French ships did worse. They fired into Charlestown itself. Men, women and children gathered on the bayfront were killed by the guns and buildings were smashed to pieces. Broadside after broadside was fired into the town and people ran for their lives to shelter wherever they could find it.

Outraged by this act of treachery, some lightly armed mer-chant ships anchored in the harbor fired their small cannon at the French warships but were battered into submission by superior firepower before they had any effect. Having done his worst, de Modene departed, leaving a shattered town and a population ranging from the richest planter to the poorest slave with an abiding distrust for the French, which would manifest itself in 1706. A diplomatic protest over this action by Great Britain to the French Ambassador in England elicited the response that de Modene's action was nothing more than a "fraternal correction". [28.1]

Pirates and Privateers

Pursuant to a peace treaty between England and Spain in 1671, the Spanish agreed to recognize English settlements in the Caribbean if the English would stop pirate attacks on Spanish shipping. As seat of the colony, the Admiralty Court sat in Nevis and captured pirates were tried here. The courthouse was the scene of these trials and the guilty pirates were marched to gallows built on the nearby beach to be hanged; hence the name "Gallows Bay."

Privateers, on the other hand, in effect were licensed pirates. In return for permission to prey on enemy shipping during wars under letters of marque and reprisal, one-third of the plunder was normally paid to the Crown. Sometimes privateers found their calling so profitable and enjoyable that they continued after hostilities ended. Their payments to the Crown then ceased and technically they became pirates.

Evidently some privateers were kept on "standby" by the Crown during times of peace and engaged in normal trade. In response to a query from the Lords of Trade and Plantations in 1676, Governor Stapleton stated that there were three available privateers in and around Nevis. One was Captain Francis, a mulatto, who commanded 100 men and a 20-gun ship. In the same letter, Governor Stapleton commented that during the last war Dutch privateers had "much molested" Nevis. Two such incidents of molestation occurred in 1674, when a Dutch privateer chased an English merchantman under the guns of Queen Ann's Fort at Indian Castle, not giving up until he had been hit several times by the fort's guns. Later that year, another merchantman was not lucky enough to reach protection and was run onto the rocks by her master rather than let the privateer take her. [29]

On August 16, 1669, a large British privateer was totally lost off Charlestown in a hurricane. Neither the ship nor its cargo has ever been found. In 1703, French privateers were active on the Caribbean. William Burt wrote from Nevis that:

> "... privateers are so thick amongst these islands that we
> can't sail from island to island but with more hazard than
> between England and this place; hardly a vessel in three
> escapes... here are some vessels loaded with sugar and
> durst not stir for fear of privateers." [29.1]

In the Leewards, privateers were commonplace up to the end of the Napoleonic wars. American privateers interfered with West Indies shipping during the War of 1812 between Britain and the United States.

In 1683, Governor Stapleton, troubled by pirate attacks on shipping, ordered Captain Carlile of the frigate HMS Francis to sail from Nevis, patrol the area, and destroy any pirate ships he might encounter. From Nevis, Carlile sailed into Danish-owned St. Thomas in the Virgin Islands and anchored alongside a large 32 -gun ship, La Trompeuse, belonging to a French pirate named Jean Hamlin. That night while the pirate ship was manned only by a skeleton crew and the rest were carousing in Charlotte Amalie, Carlile sent his sailors by longboat over to La Trompeuse. They boarded her silently, killed the crew, and burned her in the harbor.[30] Carlile sailed back to Nevis the next morning, leaving an enraged Danish Governor who complained officially that his neutral port had been violated by an English warship. More

Illustration by Nan Becker

Pirates being marched to Gallows Bay to be hanged, 1671.

than likely, the Governor had allowed the pirates to sell their ill-gotten merchandise in St. Thomas in return for a percentage of the goods traded. Shortly after this successful action, <u>Francis</u> was lost at sea with all hands.

On July 14, 1686, Governor Sir James Russell ordered Captain St. Loe of the frigate HMS <u>Dartmouth</u>, posted to Nevis, to sail to Bermuda. There he was to investigate one Bartholomew Sharpe [a notorious pirate] and if dissatisfied with his commission, was to bring Sharpe and his crew to "tryall and condemnation as pyrats." He was to do the same with any other "pyrats" he met on the way. When this was done, St. Loe was ordered to sail to Boston in New England and there contact the Honorable Joseph Dudley, President of the Council, and obtain funds to provision the ship and return to Nevis "by October next."[31]

Captain St. Loe followed his orders to the letter. On September 10, 1686, he wrote from Boston that he had apprehended Sharpe and five of his cohorts and transported them there for trial. He went on to relate that he would be late returning to Nevis, as there had been "disturbances" in Bermuda requiring the presence of his frigate to keep the peace. Interestingly, Sharpe was not hanged, but survived the trial and later wrote a book about his exploits as a pirate.

A story about a 17th century privateer who chased down a warship camouflaged as a merchantman bears retelling today. When he came alongside the disguised vessel, he hailed, "Do you surrender?" At that, the warship's gun ports flew open and her cannon were run out. Undaunted, the witty privateer responded, "If you won't surrender, then I will!"

The hanging of numerous pirates in Nevis in 1671 obviously had not put an end to them. In 1718, the Governor of the Leeward Islands informed England that he did not want to leave Nevis "for fear of being intercepted by pyrates." Pirates were a problem here through the early 19th century and if they were unlucky enough to be caught, they were almost always executed with dispatch.

Slavery and Early Life in Nevis

With sugar cultivation, slavery began on a massive scale. Its production required intensive labor. Europeans found the heat difficult to tolerate and were debilitated by such diseases as yellow fever, malaria and cholera, which were rare in Europe. In addition, many were sent here as an alternative to prison in England or as indentured servants and were not the most willing and capable workers.

Indentured servants were brought here in the earliest days. In effect, they were contract slaves. They pledged their labor for a period of three to five years in return for passage to the new world. Their labor contracts could be sold from owner to owner and frequently were, and they were often badly treated. Ship captains would sometimes convince young men to come here and then sell the contracts upon arrival to planters in Nevis.

A quasi-public company called The Society of Adventurers was founded to settle the Leeward Islands, bring over laborers, and to sell the agricultural produce of the islands in England. In many ways, the lot of an indentured servant was worse than that of a slave. In the 17th century, the proportion of European men to women was about three to one. A predictable result of the disproportionate numbers was excessive drinking, fighting and sodomy. An unexpected side effect was what was called in Nevis "the dry belly-ake," which was lead poisoning resulting from drinking excessive quantities of strong local rum distilled through lead pipes. The only known cure was moving to a cold climate — and why that worked, no one then knew. People did not realize the illness was caused by rum and lead poisoning. If a person didn't die from it, he was left so weakened that he would die from something else quite readily.

A law was passed in Nevis preventing male servants from talking to female servants and distracting them from their duties, thereby harming their master's financial interests. On the other hand, male and female slaves were imported in more or less equal numbers in order to keep the males contented. A slave's servitude was for life, and he was usually better treated, fed and clothed than was an indentured servant for that reason. Another law was passed in Nevis in the 17th century forbidding slaves and indentured servants from drinking together, as discontent could spread from one group to the other. Fewer than half the indentured servants survived their time of servitude, and when that fact became known in Europe around 1670, it became nearly impossible to find any more willing to come over. By then, the importation of African slaves had increased greatly to fill the void.

The Society of Adventurers was renamed The Royal African Company in 1660, and its charter was amended to concentrate on the importation of African slaves for profit. A monopoly on the slave trade was given by the King, hence the word "Royal" in its name. Prior to that time, most slaves had been brought into Nevis by Dutch traders. In return for the monopoly, the Company was to provide slaves at a low cost, and purchase them only as prisoners of war from the great West African slave trading forts in Guinea and Angola. In 1675, Nevis was made the headquarters for the slave trade for the Leeward Islands, and remained as such until 1730, when The Royal African Company was renamed The Merchants Company. The average number of slaves passing through Nevis during that period was 6,000 to 7,000 per year. Company statistics indicated slightly over 20% (one in five) of the slaves died during the Middle Passage journey. Nevis planters selected the best of the survivors for themselves, and the other Leewards complained constantly of Nevis' unfair advantage under this system. The slave trade was a cornerstone of Nevis' prosperity in the 17th and 18th centuries. In 1675, the population of Nevis was about 8,000, half of whom were black, and half white. By 1780, the population numbered about 10,000; 90% were black, and 10% white.

The Royal African Company lost its monopoly on the slave trade in 1696, but continued to bring all its human cargo through Nevis. From the beginning of the trade, there was a problem with smuggled slaves. Unlike The Royal African Company, the smugglers (many of them pirates) had no scruples about the origin of their cargoes. They kidnapped slaves not only from Africa, but from other islands and countries in the western hemisphere. In 1679, word leaked out that a ship anchored off Pinneys Beach carried 30 smuggled slaves on board who would be illegally landed after dark.

Phillip Lee, Speaker of the Nevis Assembly, Thomas Belchamber, a member of the Nevis Assembly, and John Starkey, Nevis Agent for The Royal African Company, sailed out in the sloop Africa, intending to seize the smuggled slaves. When the smugglers noticed Africa bearing down on them, they hailed her, "Do you intend boarding on us?" Africa responded, "Ay, by God!" With that, the two ships opened fire on each other with small arms. A boarding party from Africa attempted to go over the rail onto the smuggler's deck, and hand-to-hand combat ensued. Another merchant ship anchored nearby observed Africa's aggressive conduct, and determined incorrectly that she was a pirate. They hoisted their anchor and joined the fray, coming alongside Africa and firing into her. In the confusion, Starkey and several others were killed, and many were injured. The participants were twice brought up on charges of piracy, instigating a riot resulting in death and many lesser charges, but the cases were both dismissed for lack of evidence.

In addition to the indentured servants, Indian labor was used in the 17th century, but they perished from European diseases and overwork at such a rate that few survive in the Caribbean today. Africa was tropical and is inhabitants were thought to be more resistant to disease than were Europeans. However, Africans (like the Indians) had little resistance to European diseases, especially smallpox, and died of overwork as well. It was pointed out in the 18th century that on a

Nevis plantation where the ratio of slaves to hogsheads of sugar produced annually was one to one, the death rate of slaves exceeded the birthrate. Where the ratio was one slave to one-half a hogshead of sugar, the birthrate exceeded the death rate.

Upon arrival in the Caribbean from Africa after the Middle Passage journey, slaves were often in poor condition. In 1714, the Royal African Company agent in Nevis, John Huffam, wrote that slaves newly arrived here "were very feeble and weak at their landing and many having such a contraction of nerves by being on board and confined in irons that [they] were hardly capable to walk...."[32]

Slaves did not go gently into this long voyage. The Reverend Robert Robertson, a Scottish-born Anglican priest in Charlestown, in 1727 described the Middle passage journey as follows:

> "...the Slaves...are certainly filled with Concern and Indignation at their being forced away from their Kindred, Acquaintance, and Country, to be transported they know not where or by what Design; that the Transporters, well aware of this, and justly dreading the Consequence...find it necessary to keep all the Men hand-cuff'd, and shackled two and two, and to thumb-screw such of them as shew the least Inclination to rebel, or are suspected of it; that notwithstanding these, and great many more Precautions, the Slaves too often find ways of working off their Irons, and rise upon the Seamen, and snatching Billets of Wood, or whatever offers, knock them down, toss them over-board, turn their own weapons upon them, and mischieve them all they can; and these Insurrections are not sometimes to be quell'd without much Effusion of Blood, the Sailors being forced in their own Defence to fire upon and slaughter the Slaves..."[32.1]

He continued that two-fifths or more of the arriving slaves died while becoming "seasoned" to Nevis, and in addition others, who appeared to have adjusted well, unaccountably took their own lives or stole small boats and attempted to sail them back to Africa. It was a capital offense in Nevis at that time for a slave to steal a boat. Their birth rate did not keep up with the death rate so it was necessary to continuously import more slaves to maintain their numbers.

Robertson went on to write, "I wish from the bottom of my Heart there was never a Negro Slave more to be brought from Africa to any part of America."

It has been calculated that in the Caribbean in the 17th and 18th centuries of every five people who came here, free or slave, within five years three of the five were dead.[33] The leading causes of death in Nevis in the late 18th century were gastrointestinal disorders, tetanus (lockjaw) and "fevers", in that order. Fevers were probably malaria and yellow fever. It was written in the 18th century that in Nevis, unlike England, it was unlikely to see a "person of fifty years."

Very few records exist of life in Nevis during its 17th century heyday. However, we have been fortunate enough to find an account of an extended lawsuit between Captain John Rodney, a Nevis planter, and Governor Sir James Russell concerning the seizure and sale for debt of Captain Rodney's plantation. As the plantation itself is at issue, it is described in some detail in the surviving documentation.

Captain Rodney had been a Royalist in England and a Major in the Army. When Sir Tobias Bridge raised a force in England in 1667 to retake the West India colonies from the French, Rodney was a part of it. He was given a promotion to Captain and the force, which had sailed to Barbados, from there launched a direct attack against French-held St. Kitts. The attack was repelled and Bridge's forces retired to Nevis in disarray.

The dashing Captain Rodney made the best of a bad situation. While waiting in Nevis for reinforcements and

Map of Nevis

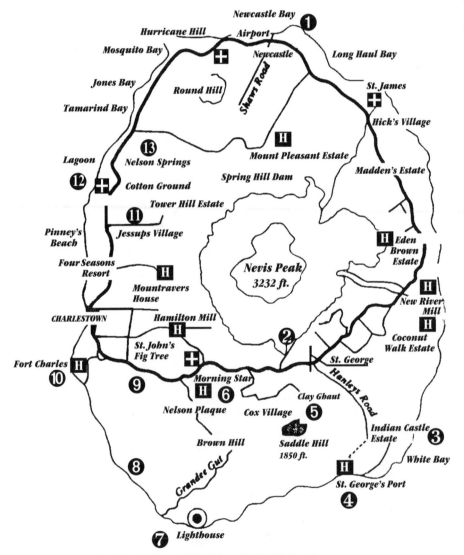

Newcastle Bay

Hurricane Hill

Airport

❶

Mosquito Bay

Newcastle

Long Haul Bay

Jones Bay

Round Hill

✚

St. James

✚

Tamarind Bay

Shaws Road

Hick's Village

Lagoon

❸

Nelson Springs

H

Mount Pleasant Estate

Madden's Estate

❿

✚

Cotton Ground

Spring Hill Dam

Tower Hill Estate

⓫

Jessups Village

Pinney's
Beach

Nevis Peak
3232 ft.

H Eden
Brown
Estate

Four Seasons
Resort

H

H

New River
Mill

Mountravers
House

H

Coconut
Walk Estate

CHARLESTOWN

Hamilton Mill

H

Fort Charles

H

St. John's
Fig Tree

✚

❷

Hanleys Road

St. George

❿

❾

Morning Star

H

❻

Clay Ghaut

Indian Castle
Estate

❸

Nelson Plaque

Cox Village

❺

White Bay

Brown Hill

Saddle Hill
1850 ft.

Grandee Gut

H

St. George's Port

❹

❽

❼ Lighthouse

Courtesy, Four Seasons Resort, Nevis; Author added historical notations.

H Historical Remains of Interest.

1 Newcastle Redoubt, probable site of Carib Indian Attack, 1667.

2 The Deodand, where Nevis militia surrendered to the French in 1706.

3 Site of battle between <u>Constellation</u> and <u>L'Insurgente</u>, February 9, 1799.

4 Probable site where HMS <u>Solebay</u> was wrecked and blown up, 1782.

5 Saddle Hill Battery, 1740. Site of Alarm Guns.

6 Battle between Nevis militia and French at Morning Star Plantation, 1706.

7 Probable site of Battle of Nevis, 1667. Site of several major shipwrecks.

8 French Bay, where d'Iberville landed 900 men in 1706.

9 Nevis militia defeated by French at Bath Plain, 1706.

10 Dutch invasion attempt repelled, 1673. Admiral de Modene's ships fire into the Fort and the town, 1700.

11 17th Century Quaker Cemetery, Jessups Village.

12 French twice bombard coastal forts, 1706.

13 Site of Jamestown, sunk under the sea, 1680. Probable site of Spanish attack on <u>Margaret and John</u>, 1620.

supplies, he met and wed a young widow, Frances Mall Richardson, who owned a medium sized plantation left to her by her first husband. He placed his brother, Caesar Rodney, in charge of the plantation and departed with his new bride for England when the military situation had settled down.

According to Governor Russell, Caesar Rodney "lived a profligate life" in Nevis and amassed large debts which he was unable to repay. At the request of local creditors, the plantation was seized and sold to repay the debts without Captain Rodney's knowledge. When word reached Captain Rodney in England, he brought suit immediately against Governor Russell, charging that the sale was made in collusion with the merchants in an attempt to deprive him of his rightful ownership of the property and the debts in question were those of the deceased Mr. Richardson.

The plantation was described as having 100 acres planted in sugar cane and was worked by 33 Negroes and Indians and four white indentured servants. In addition there were nine head of cattle and seven stills.[34] The cattle were used not only for food but also to turn an animal mill to crush the cane. The stills were used to make rum from molasses and other by-products of sugar production. On average, the plantation yielded an annual net income of 100 pounds per year. At that time 100 pounds was considered a comfortable but not princely annual income, and in today's U.S. money, would be about $70,000.00.

The lawsuit dragged on for several years and we do not know the final outcome. Caesar Rodney later became Provost Marshal of Nevis and a respected citizen. Captain Rodney's descendent, also named Caesar Rodney, was to sign the Declaration of Independence of the United States in 1776 on behalf of the colony of Delaware.

"A Sink of Debauchery"

With sugar and slavery came great profits for the planters. The Caribbean islands gained a monopoly on the production of sugar in the British Empire and prices were kept at an artificially high level — twice as much per pound as was paid in France.

In the 17th and 18th centuries the saying, "As rich as a West India planter" was commonly used in England. As an example, Azariah Pinney came to Nevis from Bristol in 1685 with a Bible and 15 pounds and died a millionaire.[35]

The Leeward Islands were separated from Barbados in 1671 and Nevis became the seat of the Leeward Islands colony. As such, it was given the nickname, "Queen of the Caribees." It remained the colonial capital until 1730 when the seat was moved to Antigua for military reasons.

Nevis during the late 17th century was rich, extravagant, and ribald. In 1671, Governor Wheler described Charlestown as "a sink of debauchery." [36] He went on to write that due largely to his efforts it had become "now as orderly as any port town in England." That was not saying much. England during those years was celebrating the end of Puritanism and life in port towns was boisterous to say the least.

As an indication of Nevis' early standing among the other Leeward Islands, it was reported in 1676 that a head tax of sugar on slaves yielded the following amounts: Nevis, 384,660 pounds; St. Kitts and Antigua, 67,000 pounds each; Montserrat 62,500 pounds; Statia, Saba and Anguilla 1,000 pounds each; and Barbuda 2,500 pounds. We do not know the per capita amount of the tax, but it indicates how rich Nevis was in comparison to its neighbors.[37]

It was noted in 1727 that a gallon of cane juice from Nevis yielded 24 ounces of sugar, while a gallon of juice from St. Kitts yielded only 16 ounces. The richness of Nevis' soil made it the leading sugar producer in the Leewards, and the richest of the islands. As early as 1640 it was said Nevis sugar was the best in the West Indies.

For a number of years in the late 17th and early 18th centuries, the value of exports from the four Leeward Islands exceeded those from all of British North America combined. Nevis itself surpassed the colony of New York for a considerable time. A 4 $\frac{1}{2}$ % export tax on sugar was in effect in all the Leewards, which produced Government Revenue for each island.

The population of the island was then twice what it is today. That is the reason the European powers spent so much time and effort fighting for dominance over Nevis and the Caribbean as a whole.

Nevis was attacked once by Spain, once by the Carib Indians, three times by Holland, and six times by France. Spain captured it once and France twice, but only for short periods or for plunder. In 1671, there were five fortifications protecting the island; seven by 1684, 11 by 1703, and 15 by 1758.

The Carib Indian Threat

We are certain that the Newcastle Redoubt was built as protection against Carib Indian attack and was designed to shelter the earliest inhabitants of the settlement. It was unsuitable for defense against a European seaward attack using ships and cannon.[38]

Similar in appearance to a small crenelated castle tower, it is believed to have been constructed in the early 17th century and is probably the oldest standing structure in the Commonwealth Caribbean. It is the only intact and unchanged fortification built for protection solely against the Indians still existing in the western hemisphere. A book written in 1730 relates that the Caribs were expelled from Nevis, St. Kitts and Antigua about 1640, so very likely the Redoubt was constucted before that year.

A secondary source from 1871, discussing the disappearance of the Caribs in Nevis, states that the growing African and European population:

> extinguished the aboriginal Carib, whose sole mausoleum is to be seen at the extreme north of the island, where the remains of a rude castellated building still exist, through which they shot their last arrows, and died

in hope of that 'bright reversion' of which heaven itself
had never bereft the savage breast.[39]

The Europeans in the Caribbean hated and feared the
Caribs intensely. Governor Stapleton in 1674 petitioned the
King to "destroy" the Caribs with French help while England
and France were at peace. Stapleton estimated the number of
Caribs ("bowmen") living in the Caribbean at that time at
1,500, with about 600 of that number being runaway or
captured slaves who had joined the Indians. He later led a
force from Nevis in 1674 which participated in an attack
against the Caribs in Dominica.

The Carib threat to the Leewards was greatly diminished
by that 1674 attack. British troops under the overall command of the English son of Governor Sir Thomas Warner of
St. Kitts, Colonel Phillip Warner, slaughtered the Caribs in
Dominica, who were commanded by his Carib half-brother.

The British had ostensibly come to conduct peace talks
and were being entertained at a banquet when the English
Warner signaled his troops, secretly landed and hidden in the
forest, to open fire on the unsuspecting Caribs. They did so
and killed as many of the Indians as they could. Warner's
own half-brother was one of the casualties.[40] The site of that
attack is today a village called Massacre.

Royal Authority had not been granted for this attack, and
much controversy was generated by it. Governor Stapleton
suffered no retribution, but Colonel Warner was arrested by
the Governor of Barbados and subsequently confined in the
Tower of London for 18 months. There is good evidence,
however, that this attack was looked on with favor by Leeward Islands residents. Upon his release, Colonel Warner
was elected to the Antigua Assembly.

In 1683, Governor Stapleton led another attack on the Caribs
in Dominica and St. Vincent, terming them "hellish villains" and
destroying 39 of their large war canoes, immobilizing them for
several years.

The Battle of Nevis — "A Wall of Defence"

A major sea battle took place at Nevis in 1667 between a British fleet of ten large vessels and a combined fleet of 30 smaller French and Dutch ships which saved the Leeward Islands for Britain.

The French had captured St. Kitts, Montserrat and Antigua and upwards of 5,000 refugees from those islands had fallen back to Nevis, putting a great strain on the island's resources. The French wisely sent all able-bodied prisoners to Jamaica. The previous year, the French attacked Nevis in a somewhat haphazard way, but failed to follow up with strong forces, costing them a possible victory.

An army was gathered in England under Sir Tobias Bridge, sent to Barbados, and from there attacked St. Kitts. The attack failed and the army evacuated to Nevis in confusion. At the same time, a naval engagement occurred in the Narrows between St. Kitts and Nevis which was inconclusive.

The able and energetic Governor of the West Indies located in Barbados, Francis, Lord Willoughby, realized immediately that holding Nevis was critical for the British. Willoughby took it upon himself to strengthen the island as best he could. He had available several warships, pressed merchant vessels into service for the Crown, and raised 1,000 troops, regulars and militia, for the relief of Nevis. In his fleet of 17 ships, he carried his troops, 2,000 muskets, cannon, gunpowder and food, all desperately needed in Nevis. His fleet set out in early July from Barbados, and near Martinique they were involved in a skirmish with some French vessels. They fought off the attackers and some of Willoughby's warships chased the French ships back to Martinique. Willoughby had to wait two days for the fleet to regroup, which worried him as it was hurricane season and there were ominous signs that stormy weather was approaching.

On the 18th of July, disaster struck. A massive hurricane caught Willoughby's fleet off Guadeloupe, only 90 miles from Nevis, and totally destroyed it. Not a single ship survived. Lord Willoughby and 1,500 men were drowned. The wreckage of his fleet and the bodies of his men were strewn along the beaches of all of the Leewards. The figurehead of his flagship washed ashore in French-occupied Montserrat and was positively identified. A handful of his men survived when their dismasted vessel was dashed ashore in The Saints and they were captured by the French.

The trajectory of the hurricane passed over Nevis and St. Kitts, where it was related that houses were cast down by the winds and the population saved themselves by going into the fields and lying flat on the ground. Almost all horned animals were killed. With the burden of refugees, destruction of food supplies and housing, combined with the loss of Willoughby and his reinforcements, the situation in Nevis was one of utter destitution. Had the French been able to raise any kind of force at all, they could have taken the island virtually without resistance. The hurricane, however, had hit the French islands as well and they were hampered in their military efforts because of it.

The French, then allied with the Dutch and the Carib Indians, saw a golden opportunity not only to take Nevis but all the Leewards permanently for themselves. The position of the British in Nevis was precarious. They were short of food, military ordnance and time.

In the meantime, the Royal Navy had gathered in England a fleet of 15 warships filled with provisions for relief of the Caribbean colonies. The overall fleet commander was Admiral Sir John Harman, who dispatched ten of his ships to Nevis under the command of Captain (later Admiral Sir John) Berry, "an expert seaman and a daring, bold commander." Berry's flagship at Nevis was HMS Coronation, a powerful 50-gun ship of the line. The several accounts of the engagement differ but it appears to have occurred more or less as follows: The enemy fleet was sighted standing for Nevis to the south of the island. Berry's squadron of ten sailed to meet them. The opposing fleet consisted of 30 smaller

French and Dutch ships, carrying an invasion force to Nevis. One accounts states that the battle occurred "in Nevis Roads," but the precise location is unknown.

The fleet Barry faced was a formidable one. Sixteen of the ships were French men-of-war ranging in size from 20 to 38 guns, commanded by General (not Admiral) de la Barre, and three Dutch men-of-war commanded by Admiral de Crynsens; one of 38 and two of 28 guns.

At the same time, the Carib Indians had massed a fleet of large war canoes on the windward side of the island. Each one carried 30 to 40 warriors. It is believed they had already made lightning raids on Newcastle and some coastal plantations while awaiting the arrival of their French allies. If the French and Dutch landed successfully on the leeward side, the Caribs were to take their shallow-draft canoes over the reefs where European ships could not go and simultaneously attack on the windward side. The Nevis militia could not effectively defend both sides of the island at once. Governor Stapleton would complain that "...the Cannibal Indians plied off during the fight to the windward in their boats, as if were hovering over their prey." This was a skillfully planned attack with a very good chance of success.[41]

The French, however, had not planned on meeting a substantial British naval force. Berry "had the weather gauge" in his favor, meaning that the wind was astern of his ships and he could attack from a favorable position. The enemy fleet apparently was not properly organized for battle and attempted to flee from the attackers and at the same time form a battle line. However, they were sailing close to the wind and were hampered in maneuvering. Berry's squadron was able to catch them and launch a strong attack before the enemy could form up.

The battle raged four hours. The first advantage went to the British, but after a time the Dutch commander was able to bring his ships up into good position. Admiral de Crynsens engaged <u>Coronation</u> with his three men-of-war; an advantage of 94 to 50 guns, but the English sent a fireship against him and he had to bear off before he could inflict heavy damage to Berry's flagship. With their fleet organized, the French and Dutch gained the upper hand for a time because of their numbers. Berry, outgunned, was fighting not only for Nevis, but for all the Leewards as well.

Because of an accident in her powder magazine, one of Berry's ships blew up and sank with heavy loss of life, increasing the enemy's advantage. [42] However, Berry skillfully used the wind and was finally able to outflank the French and Dutch, turning their battle line and driving them off. The Caribs quickly departed when the French and Dutch were turned away.

Admiral de Crynsens was very unhappy with the outcome of the battle. He accused de la Barre of being indecisive and managing the battle badly. He went on to declare that if de la Barre had been in the Dutch Navy, he would have been court-martialed for his actions. De Crynsens believed the combined fleet should have defeated Berry, and he proceeded to detach his vessels from the French fleet in disgust.

Berry brought his battered squadron back to Nevis and ordered that if the enemy was seen to be returning, a bonfire on Saddle Hill was to be lighted to warn him. It is related that a canefield in that area caught fire the following day. Mistaking the smoke for that of the bonfire, Berry put to sea again. However, the French fleet was passing Redonda and actually withdrawing to Guadeloupe, and there was no re-engagement. [43]

A grateful Nevis Council wrote the Lords of Trade and Plantations that Nevisians were:

> "...a people newly breathing from under the pressure of a dangerous and chargeable war, during which after the loss of so many of our neighbor islands, Nevis became a receptacle to all despoiled people, which lay very heavy upon us. That we did at last receive a welcome supply of ships from Capt. Berry, which proved a wall of defence and a terror to our enemies..."[44]

Berry was made an Admiral and knighted for his victory in the Battle of Nevis and a subsequent successful raid on French shipping at Fort de France, Martinique, in which over thirty enemy vessels were taken as prizes or destroyed.

In 1672, during a war with the Dutch, Governor Sir William Stapleton led a force of militiamen from Nevis, St. Kitts and Montserrat and recaptured the British Virgin Islands from the Dutch. The 80 English settlers there were removed and taken to St. Kitts.

By 1689, the French and English were again at war. Neighboring St. Kitts was divided geographically between the French and British, an arrangement which was never comfortable for either side.

The French moved promptly and attacked the British portion of the island. British civilians fled to Nevis, and in August of that year, Sir Timothy Thornhill was dispatched from Barbados with a force of 700 to relieve the hard-pressed British troops in St. Kitts. He arrived too late; the British had surrendered on July 29.

He landed his troops in Nevis and made it his headquarters. Believing he was not yet strong enough to attack St. Kitts, he led a raid on the French island of St. Barthelemy with his 700 troops and 200 additional Nevis militiamen. The attack was a success. Thornhill captured the entire island and took all of the 700 inhabitants prisoner. The women and children were sent to St. Kitts and the men brought to Nevis, together with all slaves and livestock. Encouraged by this success, he mounted another raid from Nevis against St. Martin, which was repelled by the French.

On June 19, 1690, with his troops increased to 3,000 regulars and Nevis militiamen and a naval force consisting of ten men-of-war, two fireships and 20 support vessels, he launched a full-scale attack from Nevis against the French in St. Kitts under cover of darkness. His fleet anchored at South Frigate Bay and the troops landed on the beaches there. Resistance was fierce, but by June 30, the French had been driven back to Fort Charles near Brimstone Hill. Thornhill moved his guns to the top of Brimstone Hill and bombarded the French until they capitulated on July 14. At that time France permanently gave up its portion of St. Kitts and the British took over the entire island. [45]

It would take some years, but the French would wreak terrible vengeance against Nevis for the part it played in their defeat.

The Mystery of Jamestown

The late 17th and early 18th centuries were a time of great tumult in Nevis, both natural and man-made. At 7:30 a.m. April 30, 1680, the original capital of Jamestown supposedly sank under the sea in an earthquake and tidal wave. No primary records have been located confirming it and it remains one of Nevis' mysteries.

Early maps show a town about half the size of Charlestown just south of Fort Ashby on the beach. These maps, however, were all made after the supposed sinking - some more than a century later. Yet no trace whatsoever of this town remains. It is likely that the ruins of Jamestown are not under the sea but beneath the land in the area to the south of Fort Ashby. Fort Ashby was originally built in 1701 on a point of land extending into the sea but it now lies about 100 yards inland. Thus, the land has shifted seaward by a considerable distance.

According to legend, a church sank with the town and the bell can be heard at night tolling beneath the sea when the moon is full. In reality, Jamestown was served by St. Thomas' church which was consecrated in 1633 as the first Anglican Church in the Caribbean and was located outside of the town.

In December 1687, the famous English physician and botanist Sir Hans Sloane visited Nevis for nine days. He was accompanying the Duke of Albemarle to Jamaica in HMS Assistance, a 44-gun man-of-war. He remarked that the citizens of Nevis appeared to be the least healthy he had seen in the Caribbean.

He climbed Nevis Peak in spite of danger of attack by runaway slaves hiding in the forest near the top. There he took plant samples which he later engraved on copper plates and had printed. The walk was only four miles in distance from Charlestown and easy, as the Peak was cleared for planting sugar nearly to the top.

He discussed the source of the hot water in the Bath Stream as well. Scientific theory of that day was divided on the source of such heat. One group believed it was caused by a foreign substance in the water similar to pepper in food. The second group held the water was heated by an unknown force in the earth. Sloane concluded the second theory was correct, as when the water cooled it became "ordinary water."

When he departed Nevis for Old Road in St. Kitts, he noted that Assistance required five hours to sail there from Charlestown.[46]

In 1689 and 1690 successive epidemics of smallpox, dysentery, fever and ague devastated the island and reportedly killed half the population. It was reported by the Governor that because of the number of deaths Nevis had gone from the strongest island in the Leewards to the weakest.

In 1690 a "dreadful" earthquake struck Nevis. It was written that all the brick and stone buildings in Charleston dropped "of a sudden from the top to the bottom in perfect Ruines." [46.1] These natural disasters were a portent of the troubles next century would bring.

Dutch Admiral Micheil A. de Ruyter's flagship, De Zeven Provincien, which led an attack on Nevis in 1665 during the second Anglo-Dutch war. In the 17th Century, Holland was a leading world power.

HMS Boreas, Captain Horatio Nelson, circa 1787 Painting by Vincent Neave, "Boreas bearing off St. Kitts with the island of Nevis beyond."

The French Strike Back | 5

In 1706, Nevis was twice attacked by substantial French forces. The first attack in February by 24 ships and 1,100 troops failed.

The French fleet anchored off the beach at Cades Bay and tried for five days to get boats away and land troops. Bad weather and determined fire from the shore batteries prevented a successful landing. 125 British Regulars from Antigua had been dispatched to Nevis and fought alongside the 450 Nevis militiamen. By then, Nevis had 70 mounted "great guns" — cannon firing shot of six pounds or heavier. The French withdrew in disgust from Nevis, attacked St. Kitts, took it in one day, and spent several days thoroughly plundering it.

A key man in saving Nevis was Governor John Johnson, a "bold soldier" who could neither read nor write. He had pushed hard for construction of forts and the proper arming of them. For his salary of 1,200 pounds a year as Governor of all the Leeward Islands, the crown received great value. Johnson was shot to death in 1707 by a Nevis Council Member, Captain James Pogson, in what was termed in court a duel and an acquittal resulted.

As an aside, competent legal talent was in short supply in Nevis. In 1701, Governor Sir Christopher Codrington presided over Chancery Court. He was not educated in the law and requested the Crown provide him with a qualified Attorney General upon whom he could rely. Codrington said, "...here are some little animals who call themselves lawyers, and talk to me sometimes of Pleas, Demurrers, Errors and Exceptions, which I understand as little as they do". [47]

The French returned to Martinique after the unsuccessful attack on Nevis and increased their force to 2,100 troops and 36 ships, of which 24 were men-of-war. The French land

Courtesy, Museum of Nevis History, Charlestown

commander was Pierre LeMoyne d'Iberville, a French Canadian, and many of his troops were French Canadian as well. A few years earlier he had founded the French colony of Louisiana in North America and d'Iberville Street in the New Orleans French Quarter is named in his honor. Admiral

18th century 12-pounder cannon in the ruins of Fort Charles. They were manufactured in the reign of King George III and replaced the larger guns taken by the French in 1782. These are Navy issue cannon and used an unusual flintlock firing mechanism.

Count de Chauvanac commanded the fleet.

In March, when Governor Johnson had left for Antigua with the 125 British Regulars, the French approached Nevis again from the south and left six vessels anchored off the southwest end of the island at Green Bay near Long Point. The remainder of the fleet sailed around Nevis on the eastern side and anchored late in the afternoon off Paradise beach on the western side.

At daybreak, on Good Friday, the Fleet lifted anchor, formed a battle line along the beach, and at a given signal opened fire with a thunderous bombardment by their warships of the eight shore batteries lining the beach. Most of the Nevis militia were in that area valiantly returning fire and hoping to repel the attack. When d'Iberville on the south end of the island heard the distant guns, that was his signal that hostilities had commenced. According to a prearranged plan, he landed 900 troops which he had hidden on board his six ships. There was no opposition as the main force of the militia was at Paradise Beach far to the north. Once landed safely, his troops formed ranks and marched toward Charlestown.

They were discovered near Fort Charles and some of the Fort's guns were promptly turned on them. Although greatly outnumbered, a handful of Nevis militia attacked the French column on "a hill above Bath Plain." The militia "ingaged them smartly for some time, doeing them considerable mischief." [48]

It was too little too late. The Nevis defenders at Bath Plain were soon overwhelmed by superior French forces. The invaders then attacked Fort Charles on the landward side and forced an entrance through the poorly designed gate. After brief resistance, the 35 defenders had no alternative but to surrender the Fort. No reinforcements could be expected at the Fort from the main body of the militia at Paradise Beach. These were pinned down by the French Fleet which had 1,200 additional troops on board ready to land if necessary.

When the Fort fell, the British ships in Charlestown harbor could no longer be protected from the invaders and 22 merchantmen were taken as prizes, looted or burned. The French then marched into Charlestown where they plundered and fired the town, destroying about two-thirds of it. Public records were purposely removed from the Courthouse and burned in the square, and then the courthouse itself was set ablaze.

What was left of the Nevis militia retreated to the mountain redoubt called a deodand, about 1,200 feet high, located roughly above Golden Rock Hotel. Under the command of Colonel Thomas Butler, they made a stand during their retreat in an open field at Morning Star Plantation. The 70 militiamen were overwhelmed by superior French forces, although in the fight the militia "knocked down three of their four sets of colours" [unit flags were called "colours" and during battles the opposing side aimed at the "colour bearers" who would be leading the enemy troops].

During the engagement, Colonel Daniel Smith was shot "at the back of the right shoulder through the blade bone and out betwixt the armpit and breast." When his shirt was removed for medical treatment, the loose musket ball was found. However, in spite of the gravity of the wound and primitive medical treatment of the time, Colonel Smith survived.[49]

On the way up to the deodand, Colonel Butler passed his mansion, reportedly built of mahogany wood, at Zetland. Rather than let the French take it, he burned it to the ground.

The militia secured themselves in the deodand and the French marched up and surrounded them. The notorious French "boucaniers" (buccaneers) were placed in the front lines to frighten the militia and citizens who had taken refuge there. The buccaneers were infamous for the torturing and murder of non-combatants during the pillaging of Cartegena [Colombia] in a war with Spain a few years earlier and were justifiably feared as ruthless killers.

Although the militia was prepared to "fight it out to the very stumps" as one participant put it, at the insistence of some leading citizens ("grandees"), they surrendered without firing a shot. D'Iberville's well-planned surprise attack had been a complete success and the threat of the buccaneers to the civilian population of Nevis had its desired effect.

The surprised French believed this was cowardly behavior and a loss of honor. Because of this precipitous capitulation, Nevis was treated more harshly than St. Kitts or Montserrat, both of which the French invaded and plundered during this war.

It was the intention of the French to sack the island and a major part of the expected booty was slaves. The French quickly rounded up 3,200 of the 6,700 slaves in Nevis and placed them on ships to be transported to bondage in Martinique. A majority were women and children. However, about 1,000 poorly armed and militarily untrained slaves made their way up Mount Nevis and there established a

Illustration by Nan Becker

Nevis slaves drive back attacking French troops on Mount Nevis, 1706.

defensive position. French troops advanced up the mountain to capture them, but met with fierce resistance. The French "were driven back time and again by their murderous fire." [50]

The slaves held for 18 days until the French departed from Nevis. An account of the action written by an English militia-man at the time, declared "...their brave behaviour and defence there shames what some of their masters did and they do not shrink to tell us so."[51]

The courage of the Nevis slaves was to become a legend in the Caribbean. Years later in 1757, during the Seven Years War between France and Britain, Governor Payne of St. Kitts urged his fellow Governors to allow slaves to serve in the militia. Freedmen served but slaves were not allowed to do so because of fear of rebellion. Payne declared, "The negroes stood by their masters at Nevis in Queen Anne's war while our flag was flying, they are most of them (we see) good marksmen, they don't love the French..." [52]

Angered by the unexpected resistance of the slaves, French troops rounded up the leading planters of Nevis threatening "hard usage" if they did not turn over another 1,400 slaves to their captors or pay a tribute of 30 pounds per slave. To enforce this demand, four influential planters, Charles Earle, Thomas Abbot, Joseph Stanley and Phillip De Witt, were taken hostage and transported to Martinique.

The French left after 18 days. Their intelligence had informed them a squadron of "tall ships" believed to be British was making for Nevis at top speed. The ships were actually their own, however. Shortly after they departed, a "fever" swept through their forces. Commander d'Iberville succumbed, as well as two Nevis hostages. Two more hostages were reported to be in prison in Martinique in 1715 even though the war ended in 1713.

Nevis was left a wreck. Two-thirds of the buildings, including churches, were destroyed. The Courthouse and public records were burned. Machinery and coppers were removed from sugar estates and the canefields destroyed.

Surviving stores and homes were plundered. Cannon and armament which could be removed were taken and the rest destroyed. The population was near starvation. Sugar production plummeted from 2,965 tons in 1704 to 533 tons in 1706. Nevis' sugar production would not again reach the 1704 level for more than 80 years. [52.1]

The purpose of this attack was plunder alone. By 1700, none of the European powers were really interested in adding sugar colonies in the Caribbean as sugar prices were fixed and additional production within their own Empires would serve only to push prices downward. Much more damage could be done to an enemy by concentrating powerful forces against a poorly defended island, crushing it, and then departing. Small islands like Nevis could not afford a garrison of regular troops in peacetime and whomever controlled the seas in the area could move troops at will and gain substantial booty by "blitzkrieg" raids.

Nevis' economy was devastated. The estimated losses came to one million pounds, a staggering sum in that day. In today's U.S. money, that would approximate $70 million. The British Parliament voted compensation for damages of 100,000 pounds which was dispatched to the island. As if this weren't enough, in August of 1707, a powerful hurricane struck the island and destroyed much of what had been rebuilt and replanted after the invasion.

Rich and poor alike were affected by this calamity. It was noted that "Mr. Charles Bridgewater was married not an hour before the alarm guns were fired to the best fortune here Mrs. Bartlet, but had the displeasure to see it all destroyed before he enjoyed his bride, so precarious is the riches of this world."[53]

Economic Disaster and Slave Rebellion

Nevis never completely recovered from this terrible blow. The whole island had to rebuild not only its lands and

Courtesy, Elizabeth Bilinski

The birthplace of Alexander Hamilton. Today it houses the Museum of Nevis History and the House of Assembly.

fortunes but its population as well. By 1724, the population of the island was 4,400 black and 1,100 white, about two-thirds of what it was in 1706. The sad fact was that in spite of great efforts on the part of all its people, Nevis would never regain its position as the foremost of the Leeward Islands.

With bad economic conditions, internal troubles surfaced. In 1725, and 1726, a terrible drought struck the island. In 1725 Governor Hart requested a shipload of beans from England to feed starving slaves. A Nevis plantation overseer wrote the owner in England that "The negroes are bare of cloathes and pinched in their belly..."[54] The situation was so severe that two slaves recently arrived from the Gold Coast of Africa [Nigeria] hanged themselves out of desperation, and a number who ran away perished of starvation in the mountains. Many small and medium planters were "undone" by the bad economy and left the island.

Later that year, a plot for a slave rebellion was discovered in St. James and St. Johns Parishes. Governor Hart [formerly Governor of the North American colony of Maryland], called up the militia and executed two of the alleged leaders of the rebellion by burning them alive. This stopped the rebellion before armed violence occurred. A witness wrote of the execution of the slaves, declaring that "...both dyeing deny themselves to be guilty."[55]

Governor Hart described the situation in a letter to England as follows:

On 26th Sept. (tho' in a very bad circumstance of health) I went to Nevis in a sloop with about 100 persons aboard [from St. Kitts] at my own expence, having advise that there was an intended insurrection of the negroes there, to destroy all the inhabitants: ...And having first examin'd into the intended insurrection of the negroes, who were sufficiently terryfied by the execution of two of them that were burnt... I then called the Council and Assembly together, and spoke to them in terms I thought wou'd be most agreeable, and granted them everything they cou'd reasonably desire from me...[56]

In 1727, it was written that "Nevis from being the most flourishing is, within these twenty years, become the least considerable of our Leeward Islands." In 1728, Governor Abednego Mathew declared "Nevis is a desert island compared to what it was thirty years ago." The cost of living had greatly increased and prices were double those of England. In 1737, it is reported that a strange botanical plague occurred which destroyed much of the vegetation on the island, and caused many persons to depart Nevis. No other details exist.[57]

In 1760, Nevis was criticized for indiscipline in the militia during a time when Great Britain was at war with both France and Spain. In a ringing defense, the Assembly of Nevis stated that "Discipline is the first step toward tyranny."[58] Could they have anticipated the rebellion which was to engulf the

British colonies in North America in 1776, or were they simply disinterested in the war?

In 1767, Nevis was referred to as "...a respectable but decayed mother island." Its sugar production by then had fallen not only below that of St. Kitts and Antigua, but Montserrat as well. However, during these harsh times there were some pleasant moments. The Reverend William Smith, Rector of St. John's church from 1716 to around 1725, commented in a letter to England that when approaching Nevis at night during the sugar harvest, the sight of the island was spectacular. Upon reaching Redonda, the fires in the many boiling-houses all over the island and high up the mountain were visible in the darkness across the sea and blazed brilliantly as their fire-doors were facing in that westerly direction away from the wind.

Reverend Smith related in another letter that at a party given on a Sunday afternoon following church services, as the host entered the parlor carrying "a great bowl two-thirds full of rum punch," an earthquake struck. His host proved equal to the occasion. He skillfully balanced the bowl throughout the tremblor and "spilled not a drop." One can imagine the contents of the bowl were quickly consumed in the aftermath.[59]

Saddle Hill Battery

The one factor that helped the island was the fact that sugar prices generally remained high through those trying times. By 1740, construction had begun on the Saddle Hill fortress 1,000 feet above sea level. It was costly to build and was intended to replace the deodand on Mount Nevis as a safer retreat for the population in the event of another enemy invasion. The design of the fortress was by the Royal Engineers and it was constructed by slave labor. Densely overgrown today, its stone walls extend laterally for approximately 1,600 feet and rise to heights of over 30 feet in some places. It faces southwest in the direction the French would approach the island by sea.

Three six-pounder cannon have been found in the fortress. Two were brought to the battery by the President of the Assembly in 1782 when the French captured Nevis. He briefly considered making a stand with the militia at Saddle Hill. Their fire could not reach the sea and they were later used as alarm guns. Alarm guns were usually unserviceable old cannon mounted in pairs on high points on the island and fired with a blank charge at two -minute intervals when five or more unidentified vessels were sighted standing for the island. Property owners were charged with the duty of maintaining and firing them. Upon hearing the guns, the militia were to arm themselves and report to previously designated defense points.

Drawing made by Kirt Prentice of Nevis in honor of Alexander Hamilton on an anniversary of Hamilton's birth.

One of the three knobs on Saddle Hill is called Nelson's Lookout and the walls of the fortress encircle a part of it. Nelson is reputed to have walked the walls of this fortress with his eyeglass watching for the French Fleet when he was in Nevis in the 1780's. It is said Nelson devised a mirror signaling system between Saddle Hill on Nevis, St. Kitts, Monserrat and Antigua so that in good weather, if an enemy was sighted, the British West Indies Fleet could quickly leave English Harbour in Antigua and meet them in a favorable position.

Alexander Hamilton

On January 11, 1757, Alexander Hamilton was born in Charlestown in the building which later fell into ruin but was reconstructed in 1983. It now houses the Hamilton Museum and the Nevis House of Assembly.

Courtesy, Museum of Nevis History, Charlestown

Hamilton was the illegitimate son of Rachel Faucett Levine of Nevis and James Hamilton, of an aristocratic Scottish family. His mother had been divorced some time before, but the divorce decree prevented her from remarrying, although her former husband was free to do so.

Hamilton lived here until the age of nine years and then went to Saint Croix in the Virgin Islands. As he was illegitimate, it was said he could not attend the Anglican Church School and was therefore educated at the Jewish School during his years in Nevis.

Alexander Hamilton, founding father of the United States of America, and first Secretary of the Treasury.

From St. Croix, he migrated to the colony of New York in North America to study. He later became a Colonel in the American Revolutionary Army and the first Secretary of the Treasury following Independence.

Nevis and the American Revolution

By 1756, the population of Nevis was 8,380 black and 1,055 white and by 1774, it was 1,000 white and 10,000 black. Every effort was made in Britain to persuade white immigrants to come here as indentured servants, but the white proportion of the population decreased steadily. From the mid 18th century until 1776, the income of the remaining planters and merchants remained flat or declined and there was little reason to emigrate to Nevis or any of the Leewards.

It has been calculated that in 1775, a ton of West Indian sugar brought the equivalent in today's currency of U.S. $5,000.00. On the world market in 1990, sugar sold for about U.S. $160.00 per ton.[60] In the late 18th century, William Pitt declared that four-fifths of Great Britain's overseas wealth came from the West Indies.

An account written in 1775 related that the average sugar plantation in Nevis had a yield of five hogsheads of Muscovado sugar per acre, and on average each hogshead sold for 20 pounds.[61] The American Revolution changed the situation dramatically. One planter wrote to friends in England that because of the rebellion "...we will go bankrupt or starve to death, or both." In fact, over 3,000 slaves starved to death in the West Indies between 1776 and 1783 because of the cutting off of food supplies from the thirteen rebellious North American colonies. Deaths in Nevis numbered 300 to 400. Canada tried to made up the shortfall, but lacked the resources to do so. North America supplied Nevis with corn meal, flour, salt fish, livestock and lumber. It was also the second largest market for West Indian sugar, rum and molasses behind Great Britain. A full one-third of U.S. trade volume was with the West Indies even after the American Revolution.

In 1766, Nevis and St. Kitts had the same reaction to the British Stamp Act as did the thirteen northern colonies; there were riots and 2,000 pounds worth of stamped paper was reported burned in protest. Many West Indian planters were sympathetic to the American rebels and might have joined them, but the might of the British Fleet kept any idea of independence from taking root. In 1776, the Jamaica Assembly went so far as to vote to join the American Rebels. In 1785, Horatio Nelson, at the time a Captain in the Royal Navy and on duty in the West Indies, declared "The residents of these islands are Americans by connexion and interests, and are inimical to Great Britain. They are as great rebels as ever were in America, had they the power to show it."[62]

What created immediate apprehension in Nevis was the entry of France on the American side of the war against Great Britain. Spain and Holland soon joined the American side as well. The war had drawn off British sea power to the north, leaving the Caribbean wide open to her enemies. In 1777, Nevis planter John Pinney wrote to England, "Our situation is truly alarming...Enemies all around us! I have obtained leave to raise a battery of three guns at the foot of my estate, where I shall keep all winter a nightly watch."[63]

On September 12, 1778, the following order was given to John Huggins, the gunner of Saddle Hill, by the Nevis Council:

> First, the Gunner is to remain at Saddle Hill night and day and not quit his post either Night or day without leave first obtained from the President. Second, The Gunner upon observing Five Vessels from a ship down to a sloop standing for this Island shall fire two guns at the Distance of time of two minutes between each gun, and provided such Vessels should be discovered after Sun set then the gunner shall set fire to the Pile now erected by way of Bon Fire in obedience to the General's Directions.

In 1779, French Admiral Count d'Estaing led a fleet of 28 ships of the line and 14 frigates into the Caribbean, terrorizing the British islands and taking merchant vessels as prizes, but in actuality accomplishing little. At Nevis, bad luck caught up with him. He was blockading Charlestown harbor with his fleet anchored about one and a half miles out when on September 4, a hurricane slammed into the island and his fleet. His fleet was savaged and several of his warships were lost and have never been located. Following this misfortune, he withdrew from the Caribbean and returned to France.[64]

The military installations in Nevis had been surveyed and found wanting. A petition was made to King George III for military ordnance after the "perfidious" French captured nearby Dominica, but the King turned a deaf ear. No longer the economic powerhouse it had been at the beginning of the century, Nevis was advised to request captured Dutch cannon from the British Military Governor of Statia following its invasion and destruction by Admiral Rodney.

The war drew ever closer. On January 25, 1782, the 28-gun British frigate HMS Solebay under Captain Charles Holmes Everritt was racing for protection of Nevis' guns while being hotly pursued by three French warships. Everritt ran too close to the south coast and grounded his ship. Stranded on the reef, the French ships were firing into her. Rather than allowing her to fall into French hands, he ordered the ship burned and escaped with all his crew in longboats to the shore.[65] An hour after the fire was set, it reached the powder magazine and Solebay blew up.

Admiral de Grasse Captures Nevis

Nevis' worst fears were justified when on February 2, 1782, the alarm guns in Saddle Hill Battery sounded. A great column of nearly 50 ships was heading straight for the island. It was led by French Admiral Count Francois de Grasse in his flagship, the mighty 130 gun ship of the line Ville de Paris, the most powerful vessel afloat.

De Grasse made for Fort Charles, purposely passing within range of the Fort's "old and indifferent" cannon with the purpose of intimidating the defenders. He held his fire, knowing he could smash the Fort easily. The militia knew this as well and held their fire in turn.

British iron cannon of that era were designed to fire 1,200 rounds of shot and then be scrapped. This could take years. Iron would lose its strength after the stress of many firings and guns could, and not infrequently did, blow up during a battle, especially if carelessly handled.

Enemy guns were captured and used whenever possible and there was no record of their prior usage. Most important, when funds were short or the post remote, this safety requirement was often conveniently overlooked, as it probably had been in Nevis.

De Grasse continued on to Basseterre where he anchored and sent a warship back to Nevis demanding its surrender. De Grasse's prime objective was to force the British out of Brimstone Hill Fort on St. Kitts and a necessary part of that plan was to keep Nevis under French control while the battle was fought.

With worn cannon and only 300 "indifferently equipped and poorly trained" Militia, President John Herbert of the Nevis Council determined that armed resistance would be "madness." He dispatched a delegation composed of John Pinney and James Tobin to Count de Grasse on Ville de Paris to sign a Capitulation Agreement. De Grasse gave very generous terms. The militia had to lay down their arms, swear an oath of Allegiance to the King of France, and return to their homes. They would not be forced to bear arms against Great Britain and rights of freedmen and slaves were guaranteed. Because of the serious lack of provisions on the island de Grasse took the unprecedented step of allowing British merchantmen to sail into Charlestown, discharge and load cargo, and sail out unmolested by his forces. In that day merchant vessels were almost always taken as prizes and the commanders and the troops shared the proceeds of the sale with the Crown. President Herbert gave the victorious de Grasse "ten fat sheep" for his table. De Grasse agreed to accept them as a gesture, but wrote back that any more gifts of food would displease him, as he would be forced to refuse them. De Grasse could see Nevis was in such an impoverished condition that no food could be spared. He wrote, "I am much affected at the Scarcity which your island finds itself in for the support of your negroes." [66]

De Grasse believed that Nevis was determined to avoid a ransacking such as it had in 1706 and would offer no resistance. He went so far as to propose the French occupying garrison consist of only a Lieutenant and six privates! At the same time, the 74-gun warship Le Gloreaux was sent to Nevis and 40 slaves were pressed into service to strip the island of cannon and small arms to be used against the British forces under siege at Brimstone Hill. What cannon the French did not take, they disabled.

President Herbert promptly wrote de Grasse asking that more occupying French troops be sent. It seemed an odd request to make, but Herbert wrote that the small French force might be "insulted by our negroes in spite of our utmost efforts to prevent it, as the natural ferocity of their dispositions is aggravated by lack of food, and will be further aggravated when the militia lays down its arms and if English ships appear." Undoubtedly Herbert remembered the brave resistance of the slaves 76 years earlier and feared an uprising would provoke French retaliation against the island.

De Grasse increased the number of occupying troops, placing a Garrison in Fort Charles under Lieutenant Millon de Villeroy. He also issued a proclamation that any person of color, slave or free, discovered bearing a musket, pistol, sword, cutlass or any other offensive weapon could be put to death. However, the occupation of Nevis was generally uneventful except for two incidents. A musket was discharged early one night outside Fort Charles by an unknown person and the French forces went on alert for the entire night. Millon de Villeroy complained that his troops had been fired upon in spite of no injuries being inflicted. President Herbert responded that only "unthinking madmen" would do such a thing and the gunshot must have been an accident.

Soon after the French occupation, a group of brave Nevisians defied the invaders and secretly took a small schooner at night from an outlying bay and sailed to Antigua, where they gave a report of enemy strength and military activity to Admiral Sir George Rodney at English Harbour. On her return trip to Nevis, the schooner was intercepted by the French and the occupants taken prisoner. The French claimed the Nevisians had violated the Oath of Allegiance to the King of France, but after negotiations with de Grasse they were released unharmed. The incident was termed a "misunderstanding" of the surrender terms, but in actuality de Grasse knew he had nothing to fear from Rodney as the British had no significant force available there for action against him at that time. However, when Rodney obtained a fleet later that year, he engaged and defeated de Grasse at the Battle of the Saints near Guadeloupe. It is interesting to ponder whether the information delivered to Rodney by those Nevisians assisted him in achieving his victory several months later.

5,000 French troops laid siege to and ultimately captured Brimstone Hill Fort on St. Kitts after 35 days of hard fighting. When Brimstone Hill fell, St. Kitts purported to surrender Nevis as well as itself. Nevis would have then been bound to pay one-third of the tribute the French demanded from St. Kitts. Nevis refused to pay, declaring that it had capitulated before St. Kitts had and therefore the terms of the surrender agreement did not apply to it. After much controversy and bad feeling between the two islands, the issue was decided by the Crown in favor of Nevis.

Following the loss of Brimstone Hill, Britain realized her West Indian colonies were in danger and came to terms with America, France and her other enemies and ended the Revolutionary War. Peace returned to the Caribbean—for a time. Nevis was returned to Great Britain in 1783 under the terms of the Treaty of Versailles.

Horatio Nelson

The British Navigation Acts forbade trade with all but British Empire products and ships except in emergencies. In

Nevis and the Leeward Islands, these Acts were honored more often in the breach than the observance. Horatio Nelson was sent to Nevis from Antigua as Captain of HMS Boreas, a 28-gun frigate, to enforce them. He did so with characteristic vigor and impounded four vessels anchored in Charlestown harbor flying the British Flag which were actually American vessels. The ships and cargoes were confiscated by the Crown. The cargoes belonged to Nevis merchants who brought suit against Nelson for 40,000 pounds damages. He was forced to re-

Horatio Nelson, before his marriage to Nevis plantation heiress Frances Nisbet.

main on board Boreas for two months until the lawsuit was decided in his favour.

His lack of social popularity in some quarters did not prevent him from meeting and marrying Frances Herbert Nisbet at Montpelier Plantation March 11, 1787. She was a well-to-do young widow from Nevis. John Herbert, her rich and influential uncle, was President of the Nevis Island Council and assisted Nelson in his difficulties with the lawsuit. The wedding is recorded in the parish register of St. John's church and the book is on display in the church opened to that page. It has been related that an ox was being fattened for the wedding feast in a special pen at Montpelier, but on a night just before the wedding, a hungry band of runaway slaves came upon it, took it, and ate it themselves.

Another factor which assisted Nelson socially in Nevis was the fact that Prince William Henry, Duke of Clarence and later

Illustration by Nan Becker.

The ox fattened for Horatio Nelson's wedding feast being purloined by hungry runaway slaves, 1787.

The Bath Hotel today. Built in 1778, it was the first resort hotel in the Caribbean and was visited by Lord Nelson, Samuel Taylor Coleridge and Prince William Henry, Duke of Clarence, among others.

King William IV, was a friend and gave away the bride at the wedding. Prince William Henry was commander of HMS <u>Pegasus</u> and Prince William Street in Charlestown is named in his honor. It was considered a coup to have the Prince at a social function and, of course, Nelson often accompanied the Prince. Prince William Henry was a bon vivant of the first order and was out partying virtually every night while he was in Nevis. Unfortunately, he contracted syphilis from a local lady, which probably left him with unpleasant memories of the island.

It is almost certain Nelson and Prince William Henry attended functions at the Bath Hotel. The Hotel was built by John Huggins in 1778 at a cost of 40,000 pounds and was the first resort hotel in the Caribbean. Many prominent people, including the poet Samuel Taylor Coleridge, sailed from England to bathe in the Bath Spring's thermal waters, and spent months here. The hotel remained in business nearly a century and was surrounded by lavish gardens (called the Gardens of Jericho) and carefully kept lawns. There is reason to believe that a nine-hole golf course was built there in the mid 19th century by a Scotsman. If true, it would be the first golf course in the Caribbean and possibly the Western Hemisphere.

The Ending of Slavery

Edward Huggins was the richest and most powerful planter in Nevis in the late 18th and early 19th centuries. At the time of emancipation, he was said to own over 900 slaves and many of the best plantations on Nevis. He had made profitable some which had bankrupted past owners. It is an interesting comparison to note that in the mid 17th Century the richest and most influential planter on the island was Governor Sir James Russell who owned Russell's Rest Plantation (now the Prison Farm) which was worked by 119 slaves. An inference can be drawn that as the number of Europeans on the island declined, the smaller plantations and farms were amalgamated into larger ones and more land and wealth became concentrated in the hands of fewer and fewer people.

As successful as Huggins was, he mistreated his slaves and intimidated others on the island into letting him get away with it. As an example, he forced slaves to work by moonlight manuring the fields when by consensus no one worked the fields after dark. It was also an unwritten law that no more than 39 lashes could be given a slave for punishment.

Huggins purchased a plantation in 1810 from its bankrupt owner and believed the slaves purchased with it were lazy. In

1812, he marched them into Charlestown to the public market where he brutally flogged 32 of them. One woman who was beaten died shortly thereafter, but it was officially stated that she had died of natural causes. This public whipping caused Huggins to be brought up on charges of cruelty in court at Nevis (King v. Edward Huggins). His conduct so horrified the Nevis Assembly that they passed the following resolution:

> That it is the opinion of this house that the conduct of Edward Huggins, senior, esquire, on Tuesday, the 23rd of this month, in inflicting punishment on several of his negroes in the public market-place of this town was both cruel and illegal; and that particularly, in two cases, where two hundred and forty-two and two hundred and ninety-one lashes were given, he was guilty of an act of barbarity, altogether unprecedented in this Island. That this house do hold such conduct in the utmost abhorrence and detestation; which sentiments perfectly accord with the feelings of the community in general. That this house do pledge themselves to promote the strictest investigation into this cruel proceeding, so disgraceful to humanity, so injurious to the fair character of the inhabitants, and so destructive of the best interests of the West India Colonies.[67]

A jury of his peers found Huggins innocent. The newspaper printing the Assembly Resolution was fined 15 pounds for revealing private government matters to the public. However, five magistrates who had been aware of the public flogging and had not stopped it lost their positions. This case inflamed public sentiment against slavery not only in the British Empire but in parts of America as well. Huggins was charged again with cruelty in 1817 by allegedly forcing a father to whip his own son, but was again found innocent.

The Huggins incidents were an important factor in the construction of Cottle Church. Thomas Cottle was a Nevis planter who was married to Edward Huggins' daughter Frances and owned Round Hill Plantation. He was as much the opposite of Huggins in his attitude towards slavery as a planter on Nevis could be. Cottle's reaction to Huggins' brutality took the form of building a place of worship where the races could come together. Cottle believed that the Anglican Church should allow slaves and masters to worship in the same building. At that time, it was not done because of Church inaction, so at his own expense, Cottle constructed a Church specifically for that purpose on his land. He was not a rich man and commenced construction in 1822 in the face of a severe depression in the sugar industry. Economic difficulties caused the completion and consecration of the building to be delayed until 1824.[68]

Cottle had the support and backing of the Reverend Daniel Davis of St. Paul's Church in Charlestown for this endeavor. Davis was born in St. Kitts to a planter father and went to Oxford, where he became an abolitionist. In spite of that, he returned to the Leewards and worked strongly, but quietly, for abolition in Nevis and St. Kitts. Davis conducted the first services in Cottle Church.

Cottle died in 1828 and the Church gradually fell into disrepair following emancipation. It was rebuilt by Governor Sir Graham Briggs in the late 19th century, but because of the population decline, it fell into disuse and ruin around the turn of the century.

The relations between slave and master in Nevis were generally as good as could be expected in spite of some incidents of abuse. It was written that in the latter half of the 18th century, Nevis was the best of all the Leeward Islands in that respect. Even so, problems arose from time to time from this deep social conflict. One involved the Methodist Church. Even keeping its abolitionist sentiments subdued, after a decade of success in Nevis, the Church confronted serious trouble. John Brownell, a missionary in Charlestown, wrote England in 1797:

> In October and November we had much persecution. The
> enemy raged violently. Several great men were ringlead-

ers. They frequently attended the preaching, and disturbed us by swearing, brandishing their bludgeons, swords, etc.; and forced us often to break up our meetings. I applied to a magistrate for redress but could obtain none. Our prosecuters, being encouraged, determined to set fire to the chapel and force us to quit the island. Our friends hung down their heads and did not wish to interfere; while our enemies triumphed greatly, it generally being believed that we were connected with Mr. Wilberforce in England, to support his application to abolish the slave-trade. On the 10th of November a mob came to the chapel, armed with swords, bludgeons, etc. and, while we were singing threw in a large squib [incendiary bomb], and set the chapel on fire. Such uproar, confusion, and noise, I have never heard before. However, we put out the fire; and they were restrained from doing anything further, except venting their rage on some colored people, who were obliged to flee from the island to preserve their lives. The next morning they waylaid me as I was going to a magistrate, and struck me with a bludgeon. Worse would have ensued, had not some people intervened. [69]

Mr. Brownell appeared before the Nevis Council and related his story. The Council agreed to bring the guilty persons to trial for their actions. Brownell displayed a true Christian spirit, however. He said that if the guilty persons apologized and swore not to repeat their actions, he would not press charges against them. This was done and violence did not recur.

This 18th century Lime Kiln at Coconut Walk Estate is still used today. Lime was used in refining sugar, making mortar and for fertilizer.

Constellation vs L' Insurgente
Depicts the victorious first battle of the United States Navy in the waters of Nevis on February 9, 1799.

A New Power in the Caribbean | 6

The infant United States of America was a growing presence in the West Indies. Trade between the two regions was considerable and American ships became commonplace here. Other nations noticed this fact as well, especially Britain and France. At that time one-third of all United States exports went to the Caribbean and the value of the trade increased annually.

In 1799, the United States become involved in an undeclared war against its former ally, France. Following the Revolution, France was in internal turmoil and order had broken down within the country and its armed forces. It profoundly affected the Caribbean where France was a substantial colonial power.

French warships began attacking and capturing American merchant vessels both in American waters and in the West Indies. The American Navy in 1799 consisted of only three medium-sized frigates, but President Adams believed the situation in the West Indies was so serious that he dispatched one of them, the 38 gun frigate USS Constellation, to patrol in the Caribbean. This Navy not only had never won a victory, but had never even engaged in a high seas battle. Nevis was to be the place where both the first engagement and first victory were to occur.

On February 9, 1799, Constellation, under the command of Captain Thomas Truxtun, was patrolling north of Nevis when another warship was sighted. Truxtun raised the British flag and the unidentified vessel raised the American flag.

Truxtun then raised the American flag and the other vessel raised the French tricolor flag and fired a gun to windward, indicating those were her true colors.[70]

The French vessel was the 40-gun frigate L'Insurgente, the most dangerous and daring of the French commerce raiders. She carried 419 men compared to Constellation's 321. However, Constellation's guns were fewer but heavier, giving her an advantage. All in all, the vessels were very closely matched.

L'Insurgente was commanded by Captain Berrault, who immediately close-hauled his sails and changed course to pass to the windward of Nevis, making for the Dutch island of Saba. Truxtun set off in hot pursuit. After two hours, a heavy rain squall struck the vessels and the Frenchman lost his main topmast. Constellation had been slowly gaining. After the squall, she closed even faster. After three and a half hours, one and a half miles off the southeast coast of Nevis in the area of Indian Castle, Constellation overtook L'Insurgente.

Half a cable length off L'Insurgente's port quarter with all his guns bearing, Truxtun ordered the gunners to double shot the guns and fire a rotating broadside into the enemy's hull. Berrault returned fire immediately and the fight was on. Loading with double shot decreased the velocity of a cannonball from about 1,000 feet per second to approximately half that speed. The effect was that the ball did not punch cleanly through a wooden hull but shattered the timbers, hurling splinters like shrapnel inside the vessel.

The ships had exchanged several broadsides with Truxtun going for the hull and Berrault aiming for the rigging when Truxtun made a decisive move. His ship was faster and more maneuverable than the damaged L'Insurgente, and Truxtun was able to cross her bows and rake her from stem to stern with cannon fire. The results were devastating. Berrault had assembled his considerable forces on deck, intending to board the American vessel. Cannonballs and jagged wood splinters cut through his men, causing heavy casualties and doing great damage to the vessel. At that moment, the battle turned in favor of the Americans.

The engagement continued for an hour and a quarter until Berrault acknowledged defeat by striking his colors. He lost 42 men — 10% of his crew — compared to two dead on Constellation. One of Constellation's casualties was a seaman stabbed by an officer for cowardice in deserting his post during battle. The Americans took over L'Insurgente and sailed both vessels into St. Kitts for repairs but the ships were separated by a gale. L'Insurgente was so badly damaged that she required three days to reach Basseterre. America was jubilant over news of the victory at Nevis, and was recognized as an emerging world naval power because of it.

Peace Comes to Nevis

The 19th century was to change Nevis profoundly and forever, but in a slower and less spectacular way than in the 17th and 18th centuries. Emancipation, the gradual decline of the sugar industry, and the end of the constant military threat were to come.

The Napoleonic wars in Europe had commenced and Bonaparte was determined to defeat the British at sea. The French amassed a great fleet under the command of Admiral Villenueve and sent them to threaten the Caribbean in 1805 after France had lost their colony of Haiti to rebellious slaves. In pursuit of Villenueve was Admiral Horatio Nelson, now commanding the British fleet.

Nelson was again in the area of Nevis, but did not stop here. He barely missed Villenueve at Guadeloupe, but followed him across the Atlantic. In October 1805, off Cape Trafalgar in Spain, the two great fleets met. Nelson unhesitatingly launched a brilliant and successful attack against Villenueve's combined French and Spanish fleet, considerably larger than his own. He won one of the greatest naval victories in history, but lost his life in the process.

In 1804, Napoleon Bonaparte had ordered the construction of the most powerful warship ever built and named her Imperiale. She was the Bismarck of her day, carrying a crew of 1,500 (about the same as a World War II battleship) and 132 monster cannon. Her main batteries were 48-pounders and her largest guns were 68-pounders. A 68-pounder could fire three miles with accuracy.

Imperiale, under the command of Admiral Edouard Missiessy, was ordered in 1805 to sail from France directly to Nevis. With powerful escort vessels, she anchored a mile and a half off Charlestown, out of the range of the guns of Fort Charles. While she could not be reached by the Fort's guns, she could easily hit Fort Charles and Charlestown.

Under a white flag, a longboat was sent into Charlestown where an ultimatum was presented. A ransom of 4,000 pounds had to be paid or Charlestown would be bombarded into ruin by Imperiale's huge guns. The bombardment would be followed by an invasion under the command of General La Grange, who had forces on board the ship. The town was evacuated and the population fled to the countryside. The money was quickly raised and, after payment, Imperiale sailed to St. Kitts.

The French believed Nevis had gotten off too lightly and collected 18,000 pounds from St. Kitts and 7,500 pounds from Montserrat. After this successful raid, Admiral Missiessy took most of his fleet and joined Admiral Villenueve just in time to be defeated by Nelson at Trafalgar.

On July 3, 1806, a French squadron under the command of Jerome Bonaparte, Napoleon's brother, raided Nevis and the other Leewards and captured some shipping. This was the last raid by any naval force against Nevis.

The final defeat of Napoleon Bonaparte by the British in 1815 put an end to French adventures in the Caribbean. A key man in that victory was Lord Combermere, a General on the Duke of Wellington's staff at Waterloo. Combermere later purchased Russell's Rest Plantation in Nevis from the

Stapleton family. Combermere Village and the Combermere School are named in his honor.

Nevis and the other Leewards were no longer of prime economic importance to Great Britain. In addition, the United States had formulated the Monroe Doctrine which forbade the European powers from military interference in the Western Hemisphere. The United States had by then amassed sufficient power to make it stick. American power and influence in the Caribbean was substantial and growing at the beginning of the 19th century.

Spain had declined over the years, from a position of the greatest European power in the 17th century to third place amongst them. In 1810, rebellion broke out in Mexico and spread throughout Spanish America. In 1821, Spain capitulated and gave up all her possessions in the Americas except for Cuba and Puerto Rico. Those colonies were lost to the United States in the Spanish - American War in 1898. By the end of the 19th century, Spain had ceased to be a world power and a force in the Caribbean.

During the rebellion against Spain, a Venezuelan cruiser named Brutus was lost at Nevis during a hurricane in September of 1819. It was Venezuela's only warship, and it is not known exactly where the wreck occurred or how many lives were lost.[71]

Great Britain emerged from the Napoleonic wars as the world's greatest military and economic power. With the elimination of both France and Spain as threats to the peace, and for reasons of economy, the local militia was disbanded throughout the Caribbean in 1838. All but the largest forts were abandoned or sold for building materials by the 1850's. Late in the 18th century, the British Army had organized the West India Regiment and natives of the Caribbean served with distinction in various parts of the Empire, especially in completely eliminating the old West African slave trading forts. There was a small measure of justice for what had gone before.

"Black Dogs"

Sir Hans Sloane stated in 1687 that Nevis used "blackish" sugar and Spanish coin as legal tender. Spain then possessed so much wealth that its gold doubloons and silver 8 Reale coins were used worldwide. These were the famous "pieces of eight" of the pirates and were also commonly called "dolars;" the source of the word "dollar."

Early laws in the Leeward Islands made Spanish and French coinage legal tender and assigned each of the five types of Spanish "dolars" and the French "louis" a value in English money. The laws were very strict concerning counterfeiting money. One passed in 1694, stating that:

> ...anyone found guilty of washing, shaving or counterfeiting coins shall be deemed to be a felon and shall be sentenced to death, without benefit of clergy. [72]

For practical purposes, sugar was often used as money in Nevis. Fines for breaking the law were set in pounds of sugar rather than specie until the 19th century. For example, a ship captain knowingly landing a sick person in Nevis in 1674 could be fined 10,000 pounds of sugar. Failure to have six fire buckets and a fire ladder in a store resulted in a fine of 100 pounds of sugar, etc.

For daily commercial transactions in Nevis in the 17th and 18th centuries, one was likely to find coins of virtually every nation being used interchangeably. In 1993, a rare Massachusetts Colony "Pine Tree" shilling, dated 1652, was discovered in a Nevis flower garden. The Pine Tree shilling circulated widely in the Leewards. In Nevis, by law it had a value of nine English pence, but in Antigua it was valued at only six pence. In those early years, Britain, and to a lesser extent France, simply lacked enough coinage to supply their colonies until the mid 19th century. Unlike today, coins then had an intrinsic value in gold, silver or copper. Nations could not mint them unless they possessed the necessary bullion, and paper money was unknown.

The value of English pounds was about 50% higher than the "Island Money" in use in the Leeward Islands, which were called pounds as well. It is doubtful that coins or currency were locally issued which showed this differential; a good guess would be that the difference derived from discounted pounds advanced to planters by their sugar factors in Englandwith the value expressed on handwritten slips of paper, similar to checks.

In the late 18th or early 19th century, Nevis took French coins issued for the colony of Cayenne [French Guiana] in South America or the French Windward Islands and stamped "Nevis" or the letter "N" across the face of the coin with a punch. Neighboring British islands did the same but used their own countermarks.

Examples of these coins are usually worn and are of silver or silver alloy in denominations of 1, 4, 6, 7 and 9 sous, or, as locally termed, "black dogs". There were 72 black dogs to one United States dollar and one black dog was worth about three English farthings. From time to time, these countermarked coins, especially the 1 black dog, are found locally. That particular coin is of very thin silver alloy and is often mistaken for a token. The larger denominations are pure silver.

From time to time, coins other than those of Cayenne have been found with a Nevis countermark and a number. A Spanish 1 Real coin marked "9" and the letter "N" turned up in a United States coin auction and was attributed to Nevis. The "9" stood for nine black dogs. An Irish halfpenny bearing a portrait of George III has also been found with a Nevis countermark.

Spanish pieces of eight were often cut up into eight "bits"; wedges shaped like a slice of pie, and were used as small denomination coins. On the other Leewards, these bits were sometimes stamped with the first letter of the island's name, but none have ever been found stamped "Nevis" or "N". It is

Scarcely a century after Lord Nelson was married in this house, both Montpelier Plantation and Nevis' economy had fallen into ruin because of the collapse of the sugar industry.

not certain if any exist. Countermarked Nevis coins are very rare, but not of great value to collectors. Under 100 are known to exist.[73]

The Decline of the Sugar Industry

Napoleon had failed in his dream of world domination but had mortally wounded the cane sugar industry. After losing Haiti to a successful slave rebellion, he offered a cash prize to anyone finding a way to crystallize sugar from sugar beets, which could be grown in Europe. A German devised such a process and the price of sugar fell rapidly as Europe was able to meet some of its own sugar needs.

By 1822, there was a full-blown depression in the sugar industry in Nevis. Many estates were foreclosed or sold at giveaway prices. Conditions were to temporarily improve, but over the long term, the trend was ever downward. In addition, the sugar monopoly the Caribbean Islands had enjoyed in the British Empire had been lost, forcing prices lower still. Increased world consumption of lower-priced sugar did not make up for the much lower prices being paid planters.

The individual estate production of sugar in Nevis and other small islands was inefficient and required far more manual labor than did the new central sugar factories which were being built in larger islands. Production costs in Nevis were high and prices low. By that time, most Nevis plantation owners lived overseas. Absentee ownership and resulting poor management was a growing problem. By 1830, being an overseer on a Nevis plantation was considered "... unpleasant, and indeed dangerous."[74] Slaves knew emancipation was coming and were no longer afraid to display their feelings. The abolition of slavery in 1834 put the final nail into the coffin of "King Sugar" in Nevis.

Free at Last

The African slave trade ceased in the British Empire in 1807, but slavery continued to be legal until 1834. While those enslaved wished for an immediate end to the institution, the British Government decided to do it in a gradual way and compensate the owners for their slaves. Beginning in 1817, every slave owner had to list the name, age, sex and place of birth of all slaves he owned every three years. These were called the Triannual Lists. The purpose was to have an accurate head count to go by when freedom came. It was suspected, probably correctly, that some planters with estates on several islands would attempt to move their slaves from one island to another and by doing so count them more than once and gain extra compensation.

The Triannual Lists for Nevis still exist and are quite revealing. There were a substantial number of freedmen and women who were engaged in the trades and agriculture and some of them actually owned slaves themselves; one freed-woman owned seven. When emancipation arrived, 8,815 slaves were freed in Nevis and their owners were paid compensation of 151,006 pounds. The slaves received nothing for two centuries of labor.[75]

Complete freedom did not result until 1838, however. A so-called "apprenticeship" program came into effect upon emancipation lasting until 1838. It required the slaves to work for their former owners for wages for four years until they "adjusted" to their changed circumstances. This apprenticeship could be waived by local governments and that was done in Antigua. It was retained, albeit somewhat loosely, in Nevis.

The period 1833 to 1845 was one of the most difficult ever experienced by Nevis. "Alarming" earthquakes shook the island in 1833 and about 25% of buildings and livestock were lost. Upon emancipation in 1834, planters' debts were called in, mortgages foreclosed, and credit dried up. In 1835, a disastrous hurricane devastated the island. The years 1836 through 1838 were almost totally lacking in rainfall, and fires ravaged the island. In 1837, a roaring, wind-driven blaze swept through Charlestown destroying many buildings.[76]

By 1842, sugar prices had further declined and the inefficient producers here could afford to pay only low wages to their workers. Five pence per day was the norm — if there was work available. A freedman in Virginia could earn double that amount. At that time, it cost four pence per day to feed a prisoner in an English jail. As a result, when people were free to do what they wished, there was a mass migration out to the larger islands where there was more work and higher pay. The result was a sharp decline in the island's population and an acute labor shortage.

The Nevis Council petitioned Queen Victoria to allow them to import free Africans to Nevis from British African territories. They complained that there were four vessels which did nothing but continuously transport migrating Nevisians to

Trinidad. It was proposed that these African workers would receive wages, land, and housing which would become theirs after a ten-year period. In effect, they would be indentured servants. None actually came to Nevis, however. Records do indicate that 471 persons migrated to Nevis from the Portuguese island of Madeira, and married into the local population.

Life in the New Nevis

Emancipation came at a time of a failing economy and the freed population faced living conditions which in an economic sense were worse than those under which they had existed as slaves. Poverty was a way of life, but Nevisians were now able to raise gardens and keep animals without restriction and they did so. Wages were very low when available, but people were able to subsist on agriculture and fishing in addition to, or many cases instead of, wage-paying work.

In late 1843, a series of heavy earthquakes struck Nevis. It was related in a letter that so many buildings had collapsed that Charlestown looked like a rock quarry. Very few survived intact. The Courthouse, the Treasury, the Longstone Building and the Wesleyan Holiness Manse were some which did. St. George's Church in Gingerland was so badly damaged that it had to be pulled down and completely rebuilt. Numerous buildings with date-bearing keystones show the year of construction as 1843 or 1844 as a result of this earthquake.

An unexpected benefit of the earthquakes and the fire of 1837 was that people in the building trades, especially stonecutting and carpentry, prospered and the quality of construction reached a very high level. Examples of fine quality stonework are the Courthouse, built in 1837 and the Methodist Church in Charlestown built in 1844. Former slaves took great pride in their work as they were no longer forced to do it, and it shows.

By 1852, many planters could not earn sufficient income to pay even low wages or land taxes. They complained that laborers demanded high pay and quit work at 3 p.m. In addition, the cost of goods and shipping charges had increased. One planter complained that trying to work a Nevis plantation was so vexatious and costly that he lost money and would have been glad to quit the island if he could have sold his property.[77]

In 1853 and 1854, a cholera epidemic struck Nevis killing over 800 people. It was said bodies accumulated so fast it was impossible to dig graves quickly enough to bury them individually so they were placed in mass graves. The cemetery on the north end of Charlestown was built to accommodate the victims as its location was near the hospital.

In spite of this time of hardship, Nevis issued its first postage stamps in 1861 and, in 1865, the Anglican Church

Courtesy, Elizabeth Bilinski

Ruins of the steam engine at New River. Manufactured in 1893, it crushed sugar cane until 1958.

established a library in Charlestown. In 1873, the Courthouse was badly damaged by fire, and a police constable was dismissed for negligence in allowing it to start.

One attempt to overcome the labor shortage was by installing steam machinery to crush the cane for juice more efficiently. Records indicate that as early as 1814, two beam steam engines were shipped to Nevis by the Faucett Works in Bristol. A survey made at the order of Governor Sir Graham Briggs in 1872 showed there were 19 operating steam engines in Nevis. The last working engine was at New River and it ceased operation in 1958. The abandoned machinery on many old plantations is virtually intact and may be viewed by those interested in industrial archaeology.

Animal mills and windmills preceded steam crushers, but were often used in tandem with them up to the end of sugar production. The last working windmill in the Caribbean was at Clay Ghaut Plantation in Nevis. It was disassembled in 1940, and the wooden upper works were taken to the United States Virgin Islands and placed at Whim Plantation there as part of an outdoor museum.

The Briggs Enigma

In 1879, Governor Sir Graham Briggs donated to the British Museum a very strange statue which was discovered in Nevis.[78] Briggs owned many plantations in Nevis and under his administration there was a brief period of prosperity. Unfortunately, it was only of short duration and was probably caused by the Franco-Prussian war in Europe and the resulting reduction in sugar beet production.

The statue was found on one of his properties here and is made of gray sandstone, which is not native to Nevis. It stands about three feet high and is rectangular in shape and very primitive in appearance. It shows four nude women standing together with their backs to each other and their arms linked at the elbows. Between the knees of each is a

Memorial Square and the Courthouse, Charlestown, around the turn of the century.

small human head. The hair of the women is long and curly. It is not African hair and American Indians had straight hair. This indicates a possible European origin. The British Museum has never displayed this item and has kept it in storage since the donation.

The only known similar statues are Phoenecian or Celtic. The Phoenecian examples are of much finer quality than this one, and it is closer in appearance to the Celtic examples, but not completely like them either. What makes the mystery even more intriguing is that in the 1950's, a Public Works Department employee named Ken Martin found part of a similar statue in a pile of stones at Hamilton Estate above Charlestown. He believed it was a fragment of a tombstone and carried it to the library where it was used as a doorstop for years until a picture of the British Museum statue was sent here. The newly discovered statue was then removed to the Hamilton Museum. This statue is obviously separated from a larger piece as it is chiseled off at the waist and down the back. Arm fragments and elbow fragments from companion figures are attached to the torso. Significantly, Sir Graham Briggs once owned Hamilton Estate.

Some anthropologists and archaeologists have viewed pictures of the example in the British Museum and the piece here on Nevis, and are at a loss to explain its origin or presence here. They agree it is probably not American Indian or African, but almost certainly European or Mediterranean in origin. How did it get here?

It is considered likely by many scholars that some very early European or near-eastern ships could have been carried to the Caribbean by the same winds and currents which carried Columbus and other European explorers here later on. They may or may not have been able to return home. It is not beyond the realm of possibility that a landfall in Nevis was made by some of these people very early on and all other evidence but this stonework is lost. The true answer eludes us.

Courtesy, Elizabeth Bilinski

Current day photograph of Memorial Square.

The Final Decline of Nevis

The economy of Nevis had plummeted to such depths that in 1883, the independent Nevis Government was abolished and amalgamated with St. Kitts. It would remain that way for a full century, until the Nevis Assembly was reconstituted in 1983. The once proud, populous and rich Queen of the Caribees had fallen on hard times. From the top of the Leewards in 1700, she had gone to the bottom by 1900.

The lowest point was hit in the depression of the 1930's when many of the estates were abandoned by their absentee owners and reverted to the Government for non-payment of taxes. Land was distributed to the people who subsisted marginally on agriculture and animal husbandry.

Poverty was the rule but Nevisians were proud, hard-working, and placed education as a top priority. Migration reduced the population considerably, but those who left did not forget their families and sent money home. This inflow of funds kept the island alive until the economic revival of the last decade turned it around at last.

As prosperity returns to Nevis, it is interesting to reflect on its colorful, exciting and often troubled past. In Nevis, history surrounds us and influences the present and future. As William Faulkner wrote, "History is not what was, but what is."

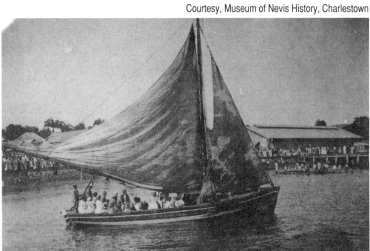

In the days of sail, a passenger vessel leaving Basseterre, St. Kitts, for Nevis, circa 1900.

Horatio Nelson was sent to Nevis from Antigua as Captain of HMS Boreas. He met and married Frances Herbert Nisbet at Montpelier Plantation in 1787.

Epilogue

This account of Nevis' colonial history ends arbitrarily at 1900. This date was selected because local records dealing with the island's early colonial period have been lost, disbursed or destroyed, and records after 1883 were destroyed when the St. Kitts Court House burned in 1982.

It is, however, the intention of **The Nevis Historical and Conservation Society** to assist in the publication of two additional books about the island's history. One will address the pre-Columbian years, and the other will portray its modern history.

Pre-Columbian Indian history will have to be developed by archaeological work and analysis. Although historical records from 1900 are available locally, they will require interpretation.

Vincent K. Hubbard
Charlestown, Nevis
October 28, 1992

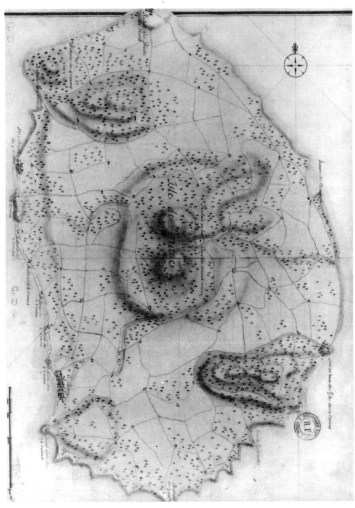

French Military Intelligence Map of Nevis, 1703. Every road and building is noted, as well as every fortification and the number of guns in each. Note the deodand on Nevis Peak ("Reduit") where the Nevis Militia surrendered to the French in 1706. Note also Jamestown on the Northwest Coast. "Newcastle" and "New River" are confused. D'Ibervilles' landing spot on the Southwest Coast is marked "Lieu De La Decente." This map was used by the French invaders to guide them in their 1706 attack.
North is to the left on the map, rather than at the top.

Bibliography

Acts of the Privy Council of England 1630-1680; Vol. 1, 1908.

An Account of the Late Dreadful Earthquake in the Islands of Nevis and St. Christopher, London, 1690.

Anonymous; A diary of an unknown person in Nevis 1806-1832, Hamilton House Archives, Charlestown.

Anonymous; A letter from Mrs Stanley's re the French Invasion of 1706, Colonial Office Records, Hamilton House Archives.

Beauvillier; Map of Nevis with details of the fortifications, 1703.

Bellin; Map of Nevis with fortifications, 1758.

Benford, Timothy B.; The 18th Century Countermarked Coins of St. Kitts and Nevis, Typed draft, courtesy of the Author, 1991.

Besse, Joseph; A Collection of the Sufferings of the people called Quakers, London, 1763.

Boxer, C.R.; The Dutch Seaborn Empire, Clays Ltd., England, 1965.

Bridenbaugh, Carl and Roberta; No Peace Beyond the Line, the English in the Caribbean 1624-1690, Oxford Press, New York,1972.

British Admiralty Map and Chart of Nevis, Made by H.M.S. Thunder, 1848.

Bullen, Frank T.; Back to Sunny Seas, Smith, Elder & Co., London, 1905.

Burns, Sir Alan; History of the West Indies, London, 1965.

Calendar of State Papers (from Colonial Office Public Records), 17th and 18th centuries.

Chatterton, E. Keble; Captain John Smith, 1923.

Coke, Thomas; A History of the West Indies,containing the Natural, Civil and Ecclesiastical History of each Island, London, 1811.

Coldham, Peter Wilson; American Arrivals in London, 1656-57, NSG Quarterly, Genealogical Publishing Company, Baltimore, 1991.

Crandall, D.R.; Historic Ordnance at Government House, Plymouth, Montserrat, West Indies, Plymouth, 1989.

Crouse, Nellis; The French Struggle for the West Indies 1650-1715, London, 1969.

Dictionary of American Naval Fighting Ships, Vol. II, 1963; Navy Dept., Naval History Divison, Washington, DC.

Douglas, Nik; A very unusual stone carving from Nevis, now in the Ethnography Section of the British Museum, Anguilla, BWI, 1986.

Gay, Edwin F. (ed); <u>Letters from a Sugar Plantation in Nevis 1723-1732</u>, Harvard University Press, Boston.

Gooding, S. James; <u>An Introduction to British Artillery in North America</u>, Museum Restoration Service, Alexandria Bay, New York, 1972.

Gordon, Joyce; <u>Nevis, Queen of the Caribees</u>, Macmillan & Co., London, 1985.

Goveia, Elsa H.; <u>Slave Society in the British Leeward Islands</u>, Yale University Press, New Haven, 1965.

Hacke, William; Map of the Western part of Nevis & part of St. Christophers, British Museum, London, 1687.

Harcourt, Robert; <u>A Relation of a Voyage to Guiana</u>, London, 1613.

Higham, C.S.S.; <u>The Development of the Leeward Islands Under the Restoration, 1660-1688</u>, Cambridge Press, 1921.

Howarth, David and Stephen; <u>Lord Nelson</u>, New York, 1988.

Howell, Calvin; <u>Nevis Handbook</u>, typed manuscript, Hamilton Museum Archives, Charlestown, 1981.

Iles, John Alexander Burke; <u>An account descriptive of the Island of Nevis, West Indies</u>, Nevis, 1871.

Jane, Charles W.E.; <u>Shirley Heights, The Story of the Redcoats in Antigua</u>, Nelson's Dockyard Park, Antigua, 1982.

Jefferys, Thomas; <u>A General Description of the of the West Indies, etc.</u>, London, 1780.

Jenkins, C.F.; Tortola, Road Town, Reprint 1972.

Las Casas, Bartolomeo; The Devastation of the Indies, 1546, Reprint 1982.

Mardis, Allen Jr.; A most cruel and bloodie fight, unpublished typescript, 1991, courtesy of the author.

Marx, Robert F.; Shipwrecks in the Americas, David McKay & Co., New York, 1987.

McConnell, David; British Smooth-Bore Artillery: A Technological Study, Canadian National Park Service.

McDonald, Forrest; The Presidency of Thomas Jefferson, New York, 1986.

Millas, Jose Carlos; Hurricanes of the Caribbean and Adjacent Regions, Miami, 1968.

Mitchell, David; Pirates, New York, 1976.

Morgan, Michael; Men of the Constellation, A History of the Naval War with France, Navy Department Library, Washington, DC, 1969.

Morgan, Michael; The U.S.F. Constellation and the Birth of the United States Navy, U.S. Naval Museum rare book room, Washington, D.C.

Morrison, Samuel Elliott; Admiral of the Ocean Sea, New York, 1942.

Muilenburg, Peter; Fate and Fortune on the Pearl Coast, Americas Magazine, 1991.

Palmer, Colin; African Slave Trade - The Cruelest Commerce, National Geographic Magazine, September 1992.

Pares, Richard; A West India Fortune, New Haven, 1938.

Pares, Richard; War and Trade in the West Indies 1739-1763, London, 1936.

Platzer, Dr. Richard; Chronology of Nevis Events, Charlestown, circa 1985.

Pomeroy, Mary; The Island of Nevis, Charlestown, 1957.

Purchas, Samuel (ed.); Harluytus Posthumus or Purchas His Pilgrims, Vol. 18, pp. 329-335, New York, 1965.

Robertson, Robert, A Detection of the State and Situation of the Present Sugar Planters of Barbadoes and the Leeward Islands, London, 1732.

A supplement to the above, London 1733.

Robertson, Robert, A Letter to the Right Reverend the Lord Bishop of London from An Inhabitant of His Majesty's Leeward-Caribbee Islands, London, 1727.

Robertson, Robert, A Short Account of the Hurricane, That pass'd thro' the English Leeward Caribee Islands, onSaturday the 30th of June 1733. With Remarks. In a Letter from an Inhabitant of His Majesty's Island of Nevis, to a Gentleman in London, London, 1733.

Robertson, Robert, An Enquiry Into the Methods that Are Now Proposed in England to Revive the Sugar Trade, London ,1733.

Rymer, James; A discription of the Island of Nevis, with an account of it's Principal Diseases, London, 1775.

St. Johnston, Sir Reginald; The French Invasions of St. Kitts - Nevis, The Brimstone Hill Restoration Society, Basseterre, St. Kitts, 1933.

Sloane, Sir Hans; A Voyage to the Islands of Madiera, Barbados, Nieves, St. Christopher and Jamaica, London, 1707.

Smith, Victor T.C.; Newcastle Tower, Nevis, Fortress Study Group, Northfleet, Kent, England, 1989.

Smith, Victor T.C.; Fort Charles, Nevis, Fortress Study Group, Norfleet, Kent, England, 1987.

Smith, Rev. William; A Natural History of Nevis, and the rest of the English Charibee Islands in America, Cambridge, 1740.

Southey, Captain Thomas; Chronological Study of the West Indies, London, 1827, (Reprint 1968).

Stapleton, Sir William; Map of the fort at Pellican Point, Nevis, 1679.

The Economist, Caribbean Review, and subsequent letters to the editor, April 1990.

Walker, G.P.J.; Cottle Church, an incedent in the life of pre-emancipation Nevis, The Nevis Historical and Conservation Society, 1990.

Watts, David; The West Indies: Patterns of Development, Culture and Environmental Change Since 1492, Cambridge University Press, 1987.

Wheeler, Richard; In Pirate Waters, New York, 1956.

Williams, William Eric; The Caribbean from Columbus to Castro, New York, 1971.

Wilson, Dr. Samuel; Dangerous Waters: Carib - European Interactions in the Caribbean, 1492 - 1700, University of Texas, Austin, Texas, 1990.

Wilson, Dr. Samuel; The Prehistoric Settlement Pattern of Nevis, West Indies, The University of Texas, Austin, Texas, 1990.

Wright, Neil and Ann; Hamilton's Sugar Mill, Nevis, Leeward Islands, Eastern Caribbean, Industrial Archaeology Review, 1991.

A wind-driven lighter in use between Nevis and St. Kitts. Called a "shallop" in the 17th and 18th centuries, this style craft has been used in inter-island travel for over 300 years, but they are rapidly disappearing today.

Footnotes

When I began this book it was not my intention to footnote it, but it grew larger and became complex in writing and footnoting was suggested. In some cases, the page numbers are not noted because I no longer have access to the materials and can't determine them. I have done my best to make the footnotes as accurate as possible, but in some cases they may not be as complete as they should be.

V.K.H.

1. Dr. Samuel Wilson has done considerable research as to the origin of of the name "Nevis" in searching for evidence of early Indian - European contact.

2. Rymer, <u>A description Of The Island Of Nevis, etc.</u>

3. Purchas, <u>Harluytus Posthumus or Purchas His Pilgrims</u>, p.329.

4. Chatterton, <u>Captain John Smith</u>.

5. Harcourt, <u>A Relation Of A Voyage To Guiana</u>.

6. Hacke, <u>Map Of The Western Part Of Nevis, etc.</u>, Discription of the island.

7. Wilson, The Prehistoric Settlement Pattern Of Nevis, West Indies.

8. Muilenburg, Fate And Fortune On The Pearl Coast.

9. Smith, A Natural History Of Nevis, p.243.

10. Millas, Hurricanes Of The Caribbean And Adjacent Regions; Marx, Shipwrecks Of The Americas, pp. 264-269; and Hamilton House Archives, Charlestown.

11. Robertson, A Short Account Of The Hurricane, etc. The book does not bear the author's name, but the words "from Robertson" are written on it by hand.

12. ID

13. Mardis, A Most Cruel And Bloodie Fight.

14. ID

15. Burns, History Of The West Indies.

16. Iles, An Account Descriptive Of The Island Of Nevis, pp.7-8.

17. Burns, Supra

18. ID

19. Calendar of State Papers [hereinafter C.S.P.], 1676, #1152.

20. Besse, A Collection Of Sufferings Of The People Called Quakers, pp.360-361.

21. Coke , A History Of The West Indies, etc., p.16.

22. C.S.P., 1671, #680.

23. Iles, Supra, p.8

24. Coke, Supra.

25. C.S.P., 1673.

26. Burns, Supra.

27. Coldham, American Arrivals In London.

28. C.S.P. 1679, #1437.

29. C.S.P. 1676, #1152.

30. Mitchell, Pirates.

31. Colonial Office Records, # 48755.

32. Palmer, The African Slave Trade, p.87.

33. Williams, The Caribbean From Columbus To Castro.

34. C.S.P., 1672, #958.

35. Pares, A West India Fortune.

36. C.S.P., 1672, #775.

37. C.S.P., 1676, #1152.

38. Smith, <u>Newcastle Tower</u>, pp. 1-2.

39. Iles, <u>Supra</u>, p.8.

40. Wilson, <u>Dangerous Waters</u>.

41. C.S.P., 1672.

42. Marx, <u>Supra</u>, p.268.

43. St. Johnston, <u>French Invasions of St. Kitts And Nevis</u>.

44. C.S.P., 1773.

45. St. Johnson, <u>Supra</u>

46. Sloane, <u>A Voyage To The Island Of Madiera, Barbados, Nieves, St. Christophers And Jamaica</u>.

46.1 An Account of the Late Dreadful Earthquake in the Islands of Nevis and <u>St. Christophers</u>

47. Burns, <u>Supra</u>

48. <u>A Letter from Mrs. Stanleys</u>

49. <u>ID</u>

50. Crouse, <u>The French Struggle For The West Indies 1650-1715</u>.

51. <u>A Letter from Mrs. Stanleys</u>

52. C.S.P., 1757.

52.1 Watts, The West Indies: Patterns of Development, Culture and Environental Change Since 1492, p. 285.

53. A Letter from Mrs. Stanleys

54. Gay, Letters from a Sugar Plantation in Nevis 1723-1732.

55. ID

56. C.S.P., 1726, #1.

57. Iles, Supra, p.11, and Bullen, Back to Sunny Seas, p.209. It is said Montserrat was also affected. It is possible that a caterpillar invasion was the cause.

58. Pares, War And Trade In The West Indies 1739-1763.

59. Smith, A Natural History Of Nevis, p.64.

60. The Economist, Apl. 1990.

61. Rymer, Supra

62. Howarth, Lord Nelson.

63. Pares, A West India Fortune.

64. Marx, Supra, p.269.

65. ID

66. Hamilton House Archives. Correspondence between President Herbert of Nevis and Admiral de Grasse regarding the surrender and occupation is complete, both in French and English, and should be of great interest to Caribbean historians.

67. Goveia, Slave Society in the British Leward Islands.

68. Walker, Cottle Church, an incedent in the life of pre- Emancipation Nevis.

69. Coke, Supra, p.21.

70. Morgan, The USF Constellation and the Birth of the United States Navy.

71. Marx, Supra, p.269.

72. Laws of The Leeward Islands, Hamilton House Archives.

73. Benford, The 18th Century Countermarked Coins of St. Kitts and Nevis.

74. Pares, A West India Fortune.

75. Goveia, Supra

76. Iles, Supra, p.11.

77. Pares, A West India Fortune.

78. Douglas, A Very Unusual Stone Carving from Nevis, etc.

Index

M

N

P Q

St. Loe, Captain, 32
St. Lucia, xiv, 3
St. Martin, (St. Maarten), xiv, 12, 48
St. Thomas, xiv, 31, 32
St. Thomas Lowland Church, 18, 49
Stanley, Joseph, 59
Stapleton, Governor Sir William, 12, 19, 28, 30-32, 43, 48, 85
Starkey, John, 35
Statia, xiv, 1, 41, 68
Stokes, Governor Luke, 27

T

Thornhill, Sir Timothy, 48, 49
Tobin, James, 69
Triannual Lists, 89, 90
Truxtun, Captain Thomas, 81, 82
Tucket, William, 23

U V

United States Navy (American Navy), cover, iv, 80-85
Venables, General Robert, 26
Villenueve, Admiral, 83
Ville de Paris, 69

W Z

Warner, Captain Phillip, 43
Wesley, Charles, 22
Wheler, Governor Sir Charles, 20, 23, 41
Willoughby, Governor Lord Francis, 25, 44, 45
Zetland, 57

*A*lthough this is a work of considerable scholarship, it is a very good and easy read; entertaining and informative. For me, the favourite is the ringing defense by the Nevis Assembly in 1760 when accused of indiscipline: 'Discipline is the first step toward tyranny.' Vincent Hubbard is to be thanked and congratulated for this rewarding serendipity.

Roger Henderson
Queen's Counsel
Temple, London, England

*V*incent Hubbard, a resident of Nevis since 1985, takes readers beyond the facts that casual visitors glean during their stay on Nevis — that Alexander Hamilton was born here, and that Lord Admiral Horatio Nelson married here. He demonstrates how the history of Nevis reflects the story of the Europeans throughout the Caribbean, where criminals, vagrants, prostitutes, and other unsavory sorts were often exiles...readers looking for a compromise between James Michener's quasi-history and the dry tomes that dominate the field of Caribbean history will welcome this lively account.

GayNelle Doll
Vanderbilt Magazine, Spring 1993